CW00549228

Dear Parents

A Gift of Love
for Families

by

Catherine de Hueck Doherty

MADONNA HOUSE
Combermere, Ontario

PUBLICATIONS
Canada   K0J 1L0

Edited and compiled by: Mary Bazzett

Cover: Jane Corbett
                    Helen Hodson

Canadian Cataloguing in Publication Data
Doherty, Catherine de Hueck, 1896-1985

DEAR PARENTS
A Gift of Love for Families

Includes bibliographical references and index.
ISBN 0-921440-44-8

1. Family—Religious life. 2. Family—Religious aspects—Catholic Church. I. Bazzett, Mary II. Title.

BV4526.2.D65 1997   248.4'82   C97-900489-6

Madonna House Publications
Combermere, Ontario
K0J 1L0

Printed in Canada

Table of Contents

iv

Foreword

This is a warning to those who are about to read this little book. As you page through its contents you may be fooled by its utter simplicity. Be careful, for if you take this book to heart, you will be plunged into a journey of faith that will be far beyond what you may anticipate.

Catherine Doherty was a prophet. She was a wife, mother, lay apostle, foundress, lecturer, writer, and an exceptionally warm-hearted woman. What comes from this book is not theory; it is her own lived reality which reveals God's formation in and through her from 1896 until 1985. She lived the catastrophic times that face all of us. She never grappled with the problems of God and man from only an intellectual point of view but allowed Our Lady of the Trinity to marinate her, through pain and joy, into revealing the prophetic answer to the difficulties we all face.

It would be wise to first read this book quickly and superficially. After that, pray and go back to the beginning with an open heart and you will realize slowly that the Holy Spirit is calling you to be part of the solution to the massive breakdown in our world, particularly the Western world.

You will find hope. You will find life. You will find a fire of faith rising up in you if you take this message deeply into your heart.

Remember that all Christian families are deeply united in the Mystical Body of Christ. We who are members of Madonna House have prayed for, supported, and loved you in a special apostolate since the beginning of Cana Colony, our summer program for families, in 1952. (See page xi.) Our commitment to families has grown in intensity as it has become ever clearer that the fate of so many hinges upon the deepening of the Christian faith of parents raising their families in this very broken and de-Christianized world.

When these talks were given, the parents receiving them had little grasp of the depth of what Catherine was saying to them. They could not comprehend how vital their responsibility as parents would be in the world today. Now we know that Christianity is dependent not simply upon the priest, the bishop, and those who are in consecrated life, but upon you and me. We are all being drawn into the fire of the Holy Trinity. Our seemingly ordinary, hidden, and humble lives are where the greatest action takes place, for we have plunged into the life, death, and resurrection of Jesus Christ.

When you have doubts, ask Catherine to pray for you. She understands your difficulties, for she lived through them and she has become a greater giver of life now that she is at home with God than she was here on earth.

Jean Fox
Director General of Women
Madonna House

Introduction

These are difficult days for families. Simply to live as a faithful Catholic family today requires great courage and commitment. In some places, the traditional family of a husband, wife, and their children living together in the same household has become a rarity. In many places, parents are heroically bearing and raising children in a culture that is inimical to human life itself.

How can followers of Jesus Christ, in whatever their circumstances, nurture their children and be supported themselves in a society where human life is cheap, where personal ambitions and material possessions are valued above everything else and where God is forgotten, rejected, or unknown? Everywhere, it seems, parents are looking for answers.

Catherine Doherty gives clear, simple answers that speak to the problems of families today. Her advice to parents is deeply rooted in the Gospel of Jesus Christ. Catherine was an expert at teaching people how to apply the Gospel to everyday life and here she does so specifically for families, drawing from her many years of experience working with hundreds of parents, as well as from her own understanding as a wife and mother, a single parent and working mom, and first and foremost, from her deep faith in God.

Catherine herself was the product of a deeply Christian home. She was born into a wealthy Russian family in 1896. The powerful Christian example of her father and mother made a deep and lasting impression on their daughter. They taught her early in life how to live the Gospel every moment of every day, even in the smallest things, even in the face of opposition.

What Catherine learned from her parents served her well throughout her prodigious life. The lessons of living the Gospel, absorbed during her idyllic childhood amidst the privileges of the aristocracy of Old Russia, were put to the test when her young life changed abruptly.

At age 15, Catherine was wed in an arranged marriage to Boris de Hueck, a wealthy Russian aristocrat seven years her senior. Shortly after, World War I began and the young bride's husband left to serve in the Russian army. Meanwhile, Catherine became a Red Cross nurse. She served the Czar's troops at the German front, dangerous work for which she was decorated for bravery under fire.

Later, she witnessed the Bolshevik takeover of her beloved city of St. Petersburg. All their wealth and possessions were seized by the communists and, fearing for their lives, Catherine and Boris left Russia, fleeing to a family summer house in Finland, where they were nearly starved to death at the hands of communists before being freed by White Russian soldiers. The couple, by then penniless, traveled to England, and later on to Canada, where their son, George, was born in 1921.

Her husband was in frail health and Catherine, to support them, took menial jobs first as a sales clerk, and later as a laundress, waitress, and maid in New York City, where she somehow stretched her skimpy salary to send money home. After a time, she found well-paying work in the lecture field, traveling across North America to give lectures for a literary agency. Meanwhile, Boris formed his own company, but it later went bankrupt in the Great Depression. Their marriage had been unhappy from the beginning. His long history of marital infidelities and emotional abuse of Catherine brought her to the brink of suicide. Their honest attempts at reconciliation had failed, their family life was completely destroyed, and Catherine and Boris went their separate ways. They later divorced and their marriage was annulled by the Catholic Church.

Catherine found herself a single parent with a small son to support. Although her position with the literary agency gave them a comfortable life, she felt hounded by Christ's words to the rich young man in the Gospel: "Sell all you possess, give it to the poor, and come, follow me" (Mt 19:21). She felt God was calling her to work with the poor and to identify with Christ in the poor by voluntarily becoming poor herself.

After a long period of soul searching and eventually receiving permission from her bishop, Catherine gave away all her possessions and wealth, keeping only enough to provide for her young son. Then, with her bishop's approval, she went into the slums of Toronto and began to live with the poor, helping them in small, humble ways. Others joined her and their efforts rapidly grew into a Catholic lay apostolate called Friendship House. Other Friendship Houses were established in Harlem in New York City and in Chicago in the 1930s and 1940s.

Catherine's son George, in the absence of a traditional family and home, was shuttled between living with his father (who lived with a mistress), boarding schools, and living with Catherine, who tried hard to make a home for him. He was troubled and rebellious in his teens and ran away from home, but eventually finished school, served in World War II, married, and became a successful businessman. Meanwhile Boris eventually remarried, formed a new family, and built a new career.

Catherine continued her work with the poor, serving the blacks of Harlem in New York City. She was a forerunner of the Civil Rights movement in the U.S. and became known for her powerful lectures on social justice. A pioneer of Catholic Action, Catherine met and became friends with others in similar apostolates, such as Dorothy Day of the Catholic Worker movement. She also became a prolific writer for the Catholic press and worked as a freelance journalist in Europe during the Spanish Civil War and the beginning of World War II.

While she was working with the poor in Harlem, she met Eddie Doherty, a famous Chicago newspaper reporter. They fell in love and, in 1943, were married by Bishop Bernard Sheil of Chicago. Catherine continued to work with the Chicago Friendship House, but many of her staff disagreed with her vision for the apostolate and, in 1947, Eddie and Catherine moved to Combermere, Ontario, in the back woods of Canada.

At the invitation of the local bishop, they began a rural apostolate there, and called it Madonna House, in honor of the Blessed Virgin Mary. People came to Combermere to join them. As Madonna House grew and more people wished to become staff workers, members of the fledgling community agreed to live in poverty, chastity, and obedience.

Eddie and Catherine also agreed to live celibate chastity as did the rest of the Madonna House staff, even though they were enjoying a deeply loving, satisfying, and fulfilling married life. For the last thirty years of their married life, Catherine lived alone in a small cabin, while Eddie stayed in their old quarters in the main building of Madonna House. Asked many years later if this unusual arrangement with her husband had been difficult, Catherine, always the passionate Russian, replied, "Brother, you don't know *how* difficult!"

In 1969 Eddie was ordained as a Catholic priest in the Melkite rite, which allows married priests. He died in 1975. Catherine died ten years later, at the age of eighty-nine. Many people consider Catherine to be a saint and her cause is now being considered for canonization as a recognized saint in the Catholic Church.

Catherine's total faith in God and her deep love for him brought her through enough struggles and hardships to fill several lifetimes. She survived the Russian Revolution, two World Wars, the Spanish Civil War, near starvation as a refugee, and untold agony, rejection, and heartbreak—all with her faith in God not only intact but strengthened, all with her love for him not only still aflame but burning brightly in a veritable bonfire. Hers was a fire of love that has warmed many souls.

Since her death, Madonna House has continued to grow steadily. The community now numbers more than two hundred members, and has twenty-two field houses which serve the poor throughout the world. According to Church law, it is classified as a public association of the faithful. Its members include single lay men, single lay women, and priests.

One of Madonna House's programs is a summer retreat for families called Cana Colony, an outreach which Catherine established in 1952. During a personal audience, Pope Pius XII had made a plea to Catherine that she never forget families and their needs. In response she established Cana Colony.

Every July and August, families from many locations come to Cana for a week of combined family vacation and retreat. Several families are received each week. It is located a short distance from Madonna House. Although there is a vacation aspect to the setting, which is in a wooded area near a lake, the main purpose of Cana is to help families share their lives in Christian community, and to find strength in Christ to live out their vocation. During the week, a Madonna House priest celebrates Mass and gives a talk for the parents each day.

The colony is named after the village of Cana, the place of the wedding feast in the Gospel, where Jesus performed his first miracle for a newly-married couple and their guests by changing water into wine, at the request of his mother Mary (Jn 2:1-10).

When Catherine spoke to the families visiting at Cana, she drew from her incredible life experience. To answer their questions, she relied upon insight and wisdom born of her deep faith in God, as well as the pain of her own life. Her words, drenched with the Gospel, are understandable to anyone, in any time, and any place. Portions of her talks to families at Cana Colony are included in this book, as well as letters she wrote to parents and meditations on various feast days for families.

The Gospel, as Catherine explained it, becomes not only visible, but alive, understandable, exciting and livable. She explained how Christianity is a viable way of life for parents and their children. Her words are enlightening, challenging and encouraging for mothers and fathers. They are a distillation of the Gospels and the wisdom of the Church, all served up with unconditional love and that rarest of human commodities: common sense.

But do not be mistaken: Catherine's words offer no "quick fix" to alleviate pain or to make living the Gospel easy. Her admonitions often challenge the assumptions and routine practices of the prevailing culture. The demands of Christ often call for a radical departure from what is called a "worldly" or "politically correct" way of life. While Catherine would be the first to take what is good from modernity and use it for the sake of the Gospel, she was fearless in rejecting what would dilute the message of Christ. When it came to the Gospel, she made no compromises, cut no deals.

Because of this, Catherine's voice is as timeless as the Gospel itself. In these pages, you will hear her speak the truth in terms that are simple, stark, and compelling. Parents who are looking for answers will recognize the truth and react to it like a Geiger counter tapping uranium. Here is the answer for every modern-day challenge for families today—Jesus Christ—and his power, his mercy, his love and his grace. Read it and feed on truth. Then go forth in faith—to nurture your marriage and your family, and to conquer every difficulty in the name of Jesus Christ.

Mary Bazzett
Editor

Part 1

Dear Parents

Chapter 1

Marriage: A Call to Love

Dear Parents,

Recently when I returned from a lecture trip, I was once more surprised at the immense hunger of people for God and the things of God, and specifically for the true search for some answers that make sense, a search upon which so many Catholic parents are embarking.

The trouble is that in this field of "answers" there is a great confusion and young parents are usually ill-equipped to find the right answers in the welter of thousands of books, lectures, television series, and radio programs to the so-called "problem" of children from babyhood up and into adulthood. Over and over again, individuals and groups ask me questions after lectures on these vital topics. Someone even suggested I start writing a book called "Dear Parents" to follow up my series of letter-writing books like *Dear Father* and *Dear Seminarian*. I thought that if I had time I would try it; and what you are reading now is the result.

As I think over all the questions parents have asked me, I see some broadly-outlined answers, for all life and all living things and beings have their beginning and end in God. God is love, and where God is, love is. So the first answer to harassed parents would be a double question: What role does God play in your life? And, how much do you really love him, and one another? Stop and think for a moment.

For you see, marriage is a *vocation*, a call of God to two people to become one, found a home, beget, bear, and raise children; and, in this glorious and very hard vocation, to become saints themselves, and to do all that is in their power to make saints of their children.

The greatest enemy of any vocation is a divided heart. Yet how many parents have a "whole heart?" Or, to put it another way, how many parents are wholeheartedly occupied with and concerned about fulfilling this vocation of theirs, as it should be filled—by serving God through it? If they were so concerned, then problem children, problem youth, and marital problems would almost vanish and, as the parents grew in holiness—which is love—these problems would vanish indeed.

What do I mean by a divided heart? I certainly do not mean adultery, or obvious physical neglect of any marital or home duty. No. I simply mean trying to straddle what cannot be straddled. For instance, trying to serve God and mammon at the same time, by putting a premium on values that are secondary —values such as money, power, position, status in the community, or social obligations, real or imaginary.

Take money. Should the wife work to get that house on a better street? Or that TV set? Or to help to pay for the car? Or should she be at home on a humbler street, content to live on whatever her husband earns, not straining after the Joneses, or trying to impress anyone but God? Is it necessary to be president of this garden club, or vice-president of that organization?

The young mother's vocation is home and children. Love seldom needs a vacation from the beloved. They are taken together. But you will say that mothers do get tired. That is true, but could that tiredness be a result of attitudes of emotional immaturity? Could it be an attitude that does not truly understand what love is, what a vocation is, where duty and joy meet in it?

Our beautiful land was built up by women just as much as by men. These women worked a thousand times harder than we do, they had many more children, and lived in much more primitive ways. Yet theirs was a land of homes. Little juvenile delinquency was known. There was love and security for the growing children in humble homes where mother was always present doing what mother should have been doing.

These women were happy doing these things. Their attitude was positive. It was not "doing chores." It was being a wife, a mother, the queen of a home. Today all this is lost. It is lost because God is not truly first but second fiddle in homes. It is much better to have time to tend a garden than to spend it belonging to a garden club.

Just mentioning these few ideas, you can see that any argument must begin with the discussion not only of the parents themselves but of their attitudes to such vital issues as homemaking, being home-bodies, and working at it intelligently and joyously.

Going deeper into their attitude, what is their final goal? Is it wealth and leisure, or is it sanctity? Let us discuss the matter more fully in our letters.

[Catherine knew full well, of course, that not every mother or every couple has a choice financially about whether she should work outside the home or not. Catherine had the experience herself of several years as a working wife and mother supporting her husband and child, and later as a working single mother supporting her child. And this was during a period of time when being a working mother was much less acceptable socially than it has become since. She understood naturally the dilemma facing parents in difficult financial circumstances and her heart was always out to them.

Nevertheless, she was ever aware, and sometimes agonizingly so, of how much it cost her son that she was not able to be at home for him. Also she was constantly in contact in her apostolate with thousands of other young people, many of them bearing the scars and pain of not having had parents available to them.—Ed.]

Chapter 2

Home: A Place to Love

Dear Parents,

In our last letter we discussed some answers to the vital question of our days—the question of relations between parents and children that seem so strained as to become almost chaotic, resulting in juvenile delinquency, in the disruption of homes and of society, of which the family is the primary unit.

Specifically, we started to discuss what broadly could be called the re-Christianization of the home. Pope Pius XII told me in a private audience I had with him in 1951 that all apostolates should help to restore the home to Christ, no matter what other aims and goals may be theirs. That is why our Madonna House Apostolate has Cana Colony for families in the summer. And that is why I have written this book.

This restoration of the home and of families begins, as we saw in the last letter, with an examination of parents' consciences. The first question is this: What is their attitude to God and to each other? We outlined briefly some searching questions about their attitude toward God. Let us now try to touch lightly on their attitude toward one another. Although this is an immense theme, I fervently hope that these few short chapters will at least start a few parents thinking.

Concerning the parents' attitude toward each other, first let's take a look at the parents themselves. To begin with, they are human beings who usually did not know each other very well, who fell in love, and decided to marry. What did they really know about this glorious, beautiful vocation of marriage, one of the hardest vocations there is?

Priests undergo long years of preparation in seminaries. So do all religious, male and female. But who gets preparation for marriage and where is its novitiate? Frankly, it should begin at their fathers' or mothers' knees, by seeing their parents' examples. Long ago, perhaps it did.

Back to the present boy and girl about to marry. They are "in love." But do they love? Do they understand that theirs is the vocation to love—and to love so well that their children will learn love by just being their children and going into the school of their love?

Do they comprehend that love is total surrender? In this case, do they comprehend that it is surrender to one another, for the love of God and each other? Do they understand that love never uses the pronoun "I" and is neither selfish nor self-centered? On the answer to these questions depends so much. Who can truthfully say, when they are entering marriage, that they know these answers?

Take the idea of rights. True, before the law, husband and wife have certain rights. This is as it should be, for life is complex and human nature is human nature, but rights are relinquished for love's sake. For instance, a nun may be an American who inherently has the right of free traveling and movement. Yet because of her love of God, she voluntarily encloses herself in a strict cloistered convent, surrendering her rights for love's sake. So it is with husband and wife, each surrendering certain rights for the sake of love.

The two become one. The man and the woman leave parents and home and cleave to one another, becoming one flesh (Gn 2:24). This means a surrender, a giving of oneself until, in truth, two are one flesh, one mind, one heart, one soul. For those who understand this—and alas, how few they are—the veil of faith becomes gossamer thin, especially at Communion, when husband and wife become one in the heart of Christ. That is where this oneness is felt most by those who believe, and believing, see.

Oneness of vocation, of love, of mind, heart, soul, and body—a man and woman bound by the soft, unbreakable bonds of an awesome sacrament—form a home.

What kind of a home is it? It truly does not matter if it is a palace, a hovel, or anything in between—good or medium, comfortable or uncomfortable by our crazy modern standards. You see, a home is not a dwelling built by hands. Rather, it is built by love, by that unity, that one-ness, that makes out of a hovel a palace of joy and peace, because the tranquility of God's order reigns in the heart of it.

Such a home, and all that goes into its making, results in mentally healthy parents and children. Here there will be no juvenile delinquency, no marital problems, nor child-parent problems, because all who live in such a home will find love, and, hence, security. These two things alone—love and security—promote that emotional health we call maturity, when the calendar years and the emotional years blend.

Chapter 3

The Healing Power of Love

Dear Parents,

We discussed in our last letter the hard, difficult and sublime vocation to love in the married state. We spoke of the oneness of man and wife—of the security which that oneness and mutual love bring to each of them, and to all their children. This loving oneness makes a home—and never mind its physical and financial trappings.

Yet across our land and, in fact, all over the world, insecurity among the young is all too apparent. We recognize it under its other medical name, neurosis. This is a disease of immaturity, emotional immaturity, which often points to a cause involving parents and home.

These insecure, emotionally immature youths marry, and the vicious cycle of neurotic parents, neurotic children, divorces, and broken homes becomes more and more apparent. It's hard to pick up a modern magazine or a popular book without coming across some diagnosis of this condition, this "cancer" that is eating out the very heart and soul of our civilization.

How can we break the vicious cycle? How can we restore the home? How can we help the growth of emotional maturity in parents and children? Knowledge is our first weapon—first knowledge of the nature of the human being, for grace works on nature. This knowledge includes a person's emotional make-up, with its needs and its checks.

Consider this. If any one of us had a broken leg, would we wish to be taken to a chapel, made comfortable there, and prayed over day and night, in the hope that the Lord would cure the break in our leg? Of course not. We would want proper medical attention: setting the break, a cast, etc. Then, after these had been given to us, we would be glad to accept helps to bear the necessary pain involved. The same would apply to any other organic sickness, because we understand the nature of the illness, at least a little.

Why, then, do we desire and even demand that psychiatry—a branch of medicine and a most respectable one —deal in religion instead of causes and effects? Religion can and will play its role in psychiatry, after we take care of it according to its nature—for here too, grace works on nature.

But what of prevention of the neurosis? Here again, we must turn back to parents. Maybe this book should be written for future parents only; yet I don't believe so. I think that good, intelligent, average people can and should face themselves and each other, and in a collective examination of conscience, find those sins of omission and commission of which they have been guilty against their "vocation to love." Truly, if all modern Catholic parents did that—the young, the middle aged, and those at the start of the eventide of life—this world would become a better place in which to live, and their children (our youth) would lose their fears, inhibitions, and sense of insecurity—in a word, their actual or incipient neuroses.

The first point of that examination of conscience should be on sins against love. Love brings the immense tranquility of God's order into all parts of life, both the conscious and the subconscious. As my psychiatrist friend Dr. Karl Stern put it so beautifully, "Love heals. Love makes man whole again. Love makes man free even from the prison of self."

What, then, are the "sins against love" that parents may commit that would result in that terrible insecurity that plagues our modern days and lives? What are their sins against each other and against their children?

The answer is stark and simple: perversion of love, mockery of it. Let me give you some examples. The indifferent husband, too occupied with his affairs and with himself, who takes his wife and her life and work for granted—he perverts love. The nagging wife, who cannot see anyone outside of the sphere of herself, who wants all things to go her way and who wants all attention and all interests to center around her—she sins against love. Selfish men and women who never think of one another, but only of themselves, and who have a bottomless urge, a sickly need for constant attention, admiration, and approbation—they break the bonds of love.

Yet these may be called, if charitably considered, the "venial sins against love." The gravest of them all, the serious sin against the vocation and love itself—God—is to channel, to demand, to wish to possess, to wish to be the end of all loves centered in a home. It is possessiveness in father or mother, or both, who want to "feed" on their children. They desire their children to "warm their cold hearts" and refuse them a life and love of their own when they have come to the age when they rightfully can and must claim it. Here you have the insecure, jealous husband and father who is even jealous of God. Here you have the possessive wife and mother who will not allow her children to be possessed even by God, or by her husband either.

If you think I exaggerate, invent, or prevaricate about this point, ask any bishop of any diocese, ask any superior of any religious order. Ask me, as a director of a lay apostolate. Ask any confessor or spiritual director. Yes, ask us. And we will tell you in one voice, that the greatest single detriment to religious vocations—and often also to vocations to marriage—is to be found in over-possessive parents, who, under the pretext that their offspring are too young, keep putting off the day of separation. They do this because they have forgotten the goal and aim, the divine purpose of marriage, which is, through mutual love, the begetting, giving birth to and bringing up of children *for God*, who co-created the children with the parents, *for his glory and the children's eternal salvation.*

They forget, too, that love never uses the pronoun "I" and that it relinquishes all things for Christ's sake. They forget that love is cruciform and cannot hold anything anyway, because its hands are nailed to a cross—voluntarily—of free choice. And in that surrender, in that effacing of the pronoun "I," in that making oneself and one's life a channel that leads all who touch it to God—away from oneself—therein lies true happiness and true maturity and true mental health.

For when all is said and done, Christ is still the greatest psychiatrist of them all. He clearly stated the principle of spiritual health which embraces mental health as well: "Unless you leave father and mother, brothers and sisters, husband and wife, you are not worthy of me" (Lk 14:26).

The single children, then, must leave the nest that is home, and father, mother, sister and brother, in order to follow Christ's call to their vocation: priesthood, marriage, religious life, or single life given to God in the world.

Even husband and wife must "leave" one another inwardly, becoming each a means for the other to reach God, and not make gods either of themselves or of each other. For even they are but means to the end, which is always God. Detachment must be at work here too, and poverty of spirit.

Let us then, in truth, make our home Christocentric, and go to Jesus through Mary, who knew so well how to love perfectly.

Chapter 4

Living Our Faith: The Way to Love

Dear Parents,

In our last letter we discussed the tragedy of modern pressures and the scourge of our days—neurosis, and the need to break somewhere, somehow, the vicious cycle of immature, neurotic adults entering the hardest vocation of all —marriage. Many are unprepared emotionally, intellectually, and spiritually for marriage, with the tragic results, seen all around us, of broken marriages and an endless line of youth, unmoored and rudderless, wandering on the sea of life without goal or port.

It was needful to point out this modern tragedy that has such deep repercussions locally, nationally, and internationally. But pointing it out is not enough. Remedies must be found to overcome the possessiveness and lack of understanding on the part of modern parents, schools, and even some parishes.

We spoke of one remedy, the acquiring of natural knowledge of a human being's mind and body functions, and the working out of human emotions, as well as their proper roles in human lives. Natural knowledge will help to clear away the mist of old wives' tales, half-truths, and untruths that have been the bane of all sane thinking through the centuries. But natural knowledge is not enough. It must be based on supernatural knowledge, which alone can free us from the bondage of fears, uncertainty, and all the allied ills—spiritual, emotional, and physical—that go with it.

Anyone who has received a Catholic education throughout his or her life is lucky indeed. Yet even these, as those who have received a partially or completely secular education, must now deepen their knowledge of God and the things of God. Some of us may have to start at the beginning, with the catechism. Others may organize for themselves a course of reading. The body of Catholic literature for lay people has grown rapidly in recent decades.

Slowly, we begin to understand that the Catholic faith is not only a matter of attending Mass on Sundays and doing the bare minimum our Church requires, for even these practices of Catholicism are but means to an end. Living the Catholic faith is a way of life that embraces every minute of our waking and sleeping hours and permeates our lives at work, at home, in school, on a date, from the cradle to the grave.

Once we understand this, a change will take place in our hearts, and the ultimate goal of life will stand out more and more clearly. We shall know, and understand well, that *we have been created to love*. We shall understand that all vocations we may embrace, including marriage, are *vocations to love*.

Love whom? God and neighbor. Why? To enjoy union with God (the Beatific Vision) for eternity. For fundamentally, we shall be judged on "how we loved," as St. Augustine said.

God then will cease to be a distant nebulous being, and become our daily companion. Little by little, we shall cease to look at life with human eyes and begin to see it with God's eyes. Then a great change and a great peace will come to us, and we will have begun to put the house of our soul in order.

With this process, knowledge and prayer must go hand in hand. And with prayer and knowledge, the reception of the sacraments by parents and children will become more frequent. The supernatural foundations will be laid for a healthy, orderly, happy Catholic life. Then the vicious circle of neurotic, self-centered existence, rendering God lip service only and spawning unhappiness for oneself and one's offspring, will be a thing of the past.

A few "how to's" will remain to be solved. These will, in reality, amount to techniques of inculcating all that went above into the family circle. Strangely enough, the first of these techniques is to return to real homemaking. That would mean mother busy only at her true role of mother, homemaker, and wife, and father working as the bread winner.

Next should come meals. It is wonderful, of course, to have a lovely modern kitchen with a breakfast nook. But breakfast nooks were not made for large families, nor are they conducive to a home atmosphere. They rather imitate the corner drug store where a bunch of skinny kids pile into a booth and order hot dogs and Cokes. No. Let the dining room of your home, or the big kitchen, if there is one, become once again the heart of the family.

Let the meal begin on time, and all the members of the family be on time for it, washed, and ready to eat good, homemade food. Maybe even the soup tureen could reappear and father relearn how to carve poultry and roasts. Let the meal be leisurely, started with prayer and ended with prayer. A thoughtful meal, where everyone watches for the needs of the others. A relaxed meal, where the whole family shares the events and happenings of the day.

The breaking of the bread is a holy and joyous occasion always—or should be. Christ used bread to feed us with himself. It was at a meal that he instituted the sacrament of the Eucharist. In all ages and in all climes, meals have had sacred connotations of hospitality, of sharing, of completion and joy. —In all ages, alas, except in our rushing, purposeless days!

Through meals children are easily taught the feast days of the year. Through them they learn much of their faith. For meals always (or almost always) accompanied God's way with man. Just consider the Passover meal and the bitter herbs and so forth, and the desert, where the manna rained down as food.

Through centuries many dishes have become symbols of feasts. You will be amazed how much you can teach your family through cooking and meals.

Reading together is another lost art. Father and mother reading aloud to the children from babyhood up should be revived. Young mothers and fathers can start teaching their children about our Catholic beliefs while reading to them at home. You may be surprised at how much *you* will learn about the faith by teaching it to your children!

Chapter 5

Combatting a Secular Culture

Dear Parents,

So many parents complain to us about their children. They come to seek advice about many things, but especially about counteracting what they call the "influence of environment." By this they mean the children next door, who are allowed to do things which they would never allow their children to do, such as keep late hours, constantly go to movies, use cosmetics, or go out with whomever they wish, whenever they wish. The list of things to fight in today's environment seems to be endless.

What is the key to combatting the prevailing culture, which is overwhelmingly secular? Fundamentally, the answer lies within the souls of parents. A searching examination of conscience must be undertaken. In a way, this searching may lead, from the worldly point of view, to dire consequences, for it may well revolutionize the lives of the parents. It has to be a thorough examination, without self-illusion, without compromise.

Together husband and wife must face themselves and see themselves as clearly as is humanly possible. Therefore, such an examination of conscience must begin with fervent prayer.

Here are some key questions that parents must ask themselves:

- What are your dreams and ambitions? What are your ideas of recreation and fun? Is your home a place where all the youngsters of the block would come in preference to movies or anything else? Is there warm understanding of youth in your home? Deep love of youth? A remembrance of your own youth, its joys and difficulties?

- As parents, do you take seriously your most awesome and holy vocation? Or do you bear with it because you have to? Is your home a place of peace and love, which are so great they radiate into every nook and corner and then spill over onto friends and neighbors?

- Is your standard of living that of keeping up with the Joneses or with Christ? Are your private conversations, your inmost ideals, lived to the hilt? Or do you say one thing—the conventional thing—and really do what *you* want? On and on, one can extend the litany of questions parents must answer to make this examination deep and faithful.

Perhaps a few examples may illustrate better what I mean:

- I knew a lady whose housekeeping was so impeccable that all the women of the neighborhood extolled her, and whose cooking was so perfect that all the men wished their wives could cook as well. Yet the strange thing was that both her husband and her children were seldom at home. Mr. X preferred to spend his evenings "with the boys," and the children could invariably be found a few doors away where the lady of the house, her husband, and her brood welcomed them happily and gave them the front living room for themselves. Mr. and Mrs. Neighbor spent much time in an old-fashioned, large kitchen, to which everyone eventually gravitated for cookies and milk, of which there always seemed an inexhaustible supply. Now Mrs. Neighbor was not a perfect housekeeper. How could she be, with youngsters running in and out all day? With toys covering tables and chairs, not to mention skates, sweaters and such? But the whole house smelled of the wondrous cookies she always seemed to be baking, and the big, inviting smile of her husband drew crowds of boys to talk about anything and everything, from fishing to dating.

• I knew another couple who made it a rule to watch television programs together. Everyone in the house was invited to comment on the program afterward. Easily, with much joking and laughter, between sandwiches and beverages, the parents taught their children to appreciate a good show. It happened quite simply. It was almost like a game. Once in a while the question was asked, "If you were Christ, what would *you* think of this show?" Very soon the children were content to be guided by the parents in their choice of TV shows. It worked miracles.

• Have you ever watched youngsters listening to an adult conversation? They even imitate the inflections of their parents' voices. I overheard a little girl of nine saying to another little one of the same age, "Oh, you mean Mrs. Y. Ho hum! She does not amount to much. Her husband is only a garbage collector." Now, where did she hear that sort of thing? I happened to know her mother, and the tone of her voice was identical. So was the content. How could the good lady hope to make that child what she should be before God, since by age nine, she had already learned to value human beings not by their worth before God, or their goodness, or their dignity as human beings, but by the silly and unimportant measure of social status or class?

• A man down the street from where I once lived beat his boy black and blue for gambling on pinball machines. Yet, he himself gambled on the stock market, and the family life was bearable or unbearable, according to stock market quotations. The boy knew full well there was something terribly unjust about this. Eventually he ran away from home. God only knows what happened to him.

Yes, an examination of parental consciences is indicated. And it must go deep, for only then can anyone counteract the baleful influences of environment. It must begin with *parents*, not with children.

If the home is Christocentric, if Mary, the mother of Jesus, is loved and cherished in it; if the avowed and openly discussed goal of the whole family is sanctity (which is the goal, or should be, of all Christians); and if life is lived and measured and evaluated against that goal, then the neighborhood environment does not matter. In fact a family like that, in any given neighborhood, will soon change the environment of their neighborhood.

Why not do this examination of conscience now—and ask Christ, who changed the world, to help you as a parent to change your home—and your neighborhood along with it!

Chapter 6

Restoring the Home to Christ

Dear Parents,

We discussed in our last letter the "worldly" environment of today in which parents find themselves while raising their children. This area of concern is followed by another which, in a way, sums up the other questions. Why was a particular home brought into being? Because two young people loved one another and came together through the beautiful portals of the most holy sacrament of Matrimony. Putting it another way: The home is a partnership of a man, a woman, and God, from whom all love and fecundity stem.

Let me repeat this, for we can never have enough clarity in this vital matter. Home is the loving place of man, woman, God, and the fruits of that love—children! Remember, it takes three to bring forth a child—God, a man, and a woman.

Home is a loving place. Where love is, God is, and where God is, all things should be his. For all have their beginning in him and hence, in him should have their ending. Life is a reaching toward that glorious ending. All life should be a school of love, a novitiate. But above all others, the home should be *the* primary school, *the* novitiate, since its very beginnings were rooted in love.

It should prepare, therefore, those who are the fruits of love—children—for all other novitiates, which are schools of love. It should serve quite naturally as it alone can as the

19

novitiate for the married state. All other novitiates draw on this first novitiate, which is the home. Without it, all others would die out. Let us bear that clearly in mind.

How wondrous and holy, then, is married life! What a tremendous responsibility too, yet what an infinite joy! But, alas, how few of us, even Christians, fully understand the duties, responsibilities, and joys of marriage and parenthood! Because we don't, we are faced with what appear to be insurmountable problems. Yet almost all of the answers can be found in that very home circle, and in its heads and foundations, the *parents*.

Juvenile delinquency, steady dating, too-early marriages, desire to escape the duties of obedience, etc., are not the problems of children, *but of their parents*.

Let us look at this statement a little more closely. Take the immense tranquility of God's order, where all things are perfectly made for a special purpose and endowed with all that is needful to achieve that purpose. Among other things, God created man and woman. To each he gave their special nature. We are not going to go into heavy theological appraisals or discussions, but look at the thing simply, as ordinary lay Catholics with a good knowledge of catechism should.

Man was created to protect, care for, and look after the woman and the children. The woman was made to bear children, to be a homemaker. If modern parents kept that simple equation in mind, they would not have to worry about their children. They would know almost all the answers that so constantly escape them now.

A child, from the very moment of its birth, needs the love, security, help, warmth, tenderness, and understanding of both parents. This is important. He also needs the immense tranquility of God's order, reflected in his daily life and routine. He needs to feel that all is well between those two beings most precious and important to him. They are his universe, emotionally, intellectually, physically, and spiritually. He needs a home, as a place where all these wants of his are taken care of, and also a state of being loved and being allowed to love, first on the natural level, then on the supernatural.

Consider modern homes, with so many mothers working outside the home or absent half the day because of the thousand social and community obligations that are utterly secondary to the needs of their children. Consider the fathers, whose goal is wealth, success, social standing and recognition, the endless keeping up with the Joneses, and anything and everything else but the primary needs of the family. Here, right here, the nature of man and woman are confused, the tranquility of God's wondrous order is broken. Is it a wonder, then, that children can't get answers to their unspoken questions in the one book they can read before their infant eyes can absorb the light of the sun—the book of parental harmony, mutual love, and the constant example of peaceful following of God's design for them and their children?

Bickering! Financial worries! Everyone, it seems, lives beyond his means. Mothers feel they have to work outside the home. They hire people to "love their children" and make homes for them. But hirelings cannot take the place of parents, no matter how grand they are.

The girl, as she grows up, is not shown the ways of womankind. She is not allowed to help in the homemaking arts. Instead, she is encouraged to "make something of herself," to study, to shine scholastically. This would be okay if all other things that belong to her nature as a woman-to-be were also given to her. But they are not. So the novitiate, the school of love that the home is because it is a home, the loving place of God and man, ceases to be that and becomes a place from which the child wants to escape. The peace of God has been rejected there by her parents. To where is she going to escape? The answers are clear: into steady dating, an attempt to find some sort of loving security; into a search for what has been denied her at the very roots of life.

Some answers to the problems of today's families are hidden deeply. They are hidden in the breaking up of God's pattern for holy married life, in his being relegated to second place, with all the tensions, tragedies, and miseries that follow.

Neither poverty nor riches has anything to do with all this. Love has—love of parents for God and each other. Obedience to his commandments of love. These reveal the answers in big, legible letters to every mother and father. Is the home a loving place of man, woman, and God? Is it functioning according to the tranquility of God's loving order? Or is it not? Each set of parents must answer these questions for themselves. If they do, truthfully, lovingly, and without fears, they will be able to answer all other questions their children may ask them, for they will have graduated from their own school of love and love knows all answers.

To synthesize, the answers to questions put to us by bewildered parents all over the U.S. and Canada lie in this: *the parents' full and complete living of their most holy vocation to love in the married state.* They do this through the great power that is theirs in the sacrament of Matrimony. If they do this, then most of their questions won't have to be asked. The children will understand love, and then the little-needed academic details on sex, which is the chalice of the sacrament of Matrimony, will be answered easily and happily too.

Chapter 7

Going Deeper

Dear Parents,

You will remember in chapter 5 we were discussing an examination of conscience. It was not quite the usual type of examination, for it was to be done together, by both husband and wife. By now you are already used to making such examinations, for, as we said, the first is made on the fundamentals of our holy faith and their implementation in the daily life of the family—morning and evening prayers, grace before and after meals, good Catholic reading, etc.

This time we will have to go a little deeper. What are the conversations about around your house? Is mother always complaining of her lot, disparaging housework and all the chores of the daily family grind, giving a definite and distorted impression of the sublime vocation of marriage, an impression that may well affect the lives of the children? The impressions of childhood days make or unmake the adult.

Is there much gossip with friends? Are friends or neighbors discussed uncharitably or sarcastically? Is father forever placing before the children a materialistic standard? Are father and mother eternally trying to keep up with those mythical Joneses? Are the children forbidden associations with other children because of race, color, or creed, social or financial levels, or other worldly standards?

Are priests and religious discussed with a sort of "tongue in cheek" attitude? Are vocations to the priesthood and religious life spoken of as strange and unsuitable to our times, or are they set up as the greatest gifts God can give? Are they spoken of hopefully, prayerfully, and with reverence?

Is the interest of the parents, and, through them, the interest of the whole family, directed to those forms of Catholic Action which are suitable to their state in life, especially those which take in the whole family? And are the broader aspects of action as lay people studied and spoken about?

Is the home and its entity centered on Christ? How deep is its devotion to Mary, the gracious Mother of God? Do parents realize that the sole reason they are parents is to become saints in the glorious vocation of holy matrimony? Do they teach their children that this is the sole goal of their life on earth—to become saints?

Are the children encouraged to seek their right vocations as their adulthood approaches? Are the parents ready to "let go" of their children when the time comes—between eighteen and twenty-one years of age? Or do they love their children with a possessive, selfish, self-centered love?

Are parents well aware of their duties to their children? Do children really know their obligations to their parents, not as the worldly standard would have it, but as God has established it?

Are all family problems and decisions discussed and solved as God would wish them to be solved? Do parents look at life with God's eyes, or with the blurred, cynical eyes of the world? Is sanctity the real goal of life, or a mere secondary one?

You see, dear friends, such an examination of conscience really bites deep. We live in a secular world. What is secularism? It is divorcing God from our daily life. We modern Catholics live in such an age of secularism that it is hard for us even to realize how far we have drifted into the heart of that secularism, that divorce.

Take, for instance, the question of the duty of parents to children, or children to parents. Let's begin at the beginning.

You have fallen in love. You marry. In most cases, you will have children. They are the fruit of your love for each other and for God.

Those children owe you gratitude for the gift of life, and hence their opportunity for life eternal, and the Beatific Vision. They must, in gratitude and charity, "lay down their lives for you," if need be. Should *you* someday need their help, they must forego any other vocation to devote themselves to assisting and caring for you *but on one condition only—that your need is true, not imaginary*. In our day, in this age of state welfare, old age pensions, union pension plans, hospitalization plans, and insurance plus social security, such a genuine need of parents is hard to imagine. It must be your fundamental need of food, clothing and shelter, plus urgent medical care that forces the children to give up their vocations and look after you.

The parents' duty toward their children is greater. They owe them food, shelter, clothing and education according to their state in life, and a full and thorough knowledge of God and the things of God. For these, no child has to "pay"—in time, in gratitude, or in kind. It would be most unfair to hold filial duty and gratitude for these things over their heads when they are ready to leave the parental roof for their own vocations in life.

Obedience of children to parents, until they are of age, must be unquestioning. But once they have come of age, they must be freed from such childish obedience. They must seek advice, yes, but they do not necessarily have to follow it.

Both parents and children must understand that home is but the novitiate of life, the school of sanctity. Parents should understand well that they are but custodians, stewards of God, for their children, and that when God calls these children to other vocations and other fields, they must depart easily, joyously, and with the joyous consent of their parents.

Chapter 8

Letting Go

Dear Parents,

Today I would like to treat a subject that is most vital to all parents—namely, the subject of vocations. Over the years I have observed more than ten thousand young people who have passed through Friendship House and Madonna House, many of whom are seeking their vocations in life.

In our days of vocational needs that press the Church on all sides, many vocations are lost because we do not evaluate subjects as whole people—especially as to their emotional ages. It is quite possible for someone to be twenty-five years of age, have a Ph.D., and be emotionally around twelve or fourteen years of age! Emotional immaturity can cause a thousand conflicts within an individual. A little patience, much understanding of human nature, and maybe a check-up by a qualified doctor or psychiatrist and a lost vocation can be found again. Neurosis, the disease of the century, is, in its mild form, just that —emotional immaturity.

What contributes to it? That would make a wonderful study for those interested in vocations and in parishioners. And it would lighten the burden of a parish priest and his assistants a hundredfold if they did their share in breaking the vicious circle responsible for most of this emotional immaturity, which often has its birth in the home.

For it is the love and security that the home gives that make the child a healthy person, emotionally speaking. Where parents love each other, where the peace and love of God are in the home, where God takes first place, a child will grow into a healthy individual, mentally, emotionally, and probably physically. And the parish and religious orders, as well as the community at large, will benefit enormously from the resulting vocations to priesthood, religious life, marriage and single life.

Love and security are synonymous. Where there is love, there always is security. But when love is spoken of, it has to be defined. It must be mature, certain, ingenious, watchful, delicate, and without fears. Otherwise it is not love, but a tragic substitute.

Now take parents who are possessive and who will not let go, who blanch at the idea of their daughter becoming a nun, their son a priest or a brother, and who fear their children will marry "early," and thus "desert" poor mom and pop! Such parents often cause the neuroses of their children. By the time the children grow up, those neuroses will be full-blown and will ruin them—unless they are lucky enough to encounter some heart that understands.

How many guilt complexes were begotten from a misunderstood sense of duty that chained young people to parents! How often did they wish they had never seen the inside of college dorms! Half their lives have been spent listening to what they owe their parents for their education! Some parents imply they slaved and mortgaged their very roofs just to give their children "the very best." Did they have to do it? Were they driven by their ambitions or by the mistaken idea that a manual labor job is socially unacceptable? What sort of jobs did *they* have before they came into wealth? A child is naturally proud of his father, whether he is a truck driver, a carpenter, or a banker. Why, by implication, let him believe he must have something better? Is it better? If so, why? Because everyone feels that way? How does God feel about it?

Of course no generalization is possible, for each case is unique. Yet, there are guides I love to remember. If applied to modern life, they would cut neuroses by more than half. They are as follows:

• For the privilege of being man and wife, with all the joys and prerogatives that apply to this holy vocation, we must beget, bear and rear children for the honor and glory of God, our sanctification, and theirs.

• Parents owe their children the gift of life, food, shelter, clothing, and education, *according to their state in life and their financial standing,* plus of course that intangible formation of character that is the product of a Christian home. They have been loaned, these children, by God, in order for parents to give them back to him as saints of heaven. Therefore "education" primarily includes everything that will make them *know, love and serve God better.*

• The child owes the parents nothing for food, shelter, clothing and education. But, he owes everything for the gift of life. Until maturity and coming of age, he owes them obedience. Always he must listen respectfully and carefully to the advice of his parents, for they have a special grace to advise their children. *If and when* parents are destitute or are ill and helpless, the child repays the gift of life, even by laying down his life. But *only then.*

• Parents must understand they do not "possess" their children. God does. And woe to the father or mother who interferes with vocations, especially religious ones. (For they reject God for a son-in-law or a daughter-in-law!)

• Briefly, we rear our children in order to let go of them and to let them go forth from us, that they may embrace the vocation to which God calls them.

Pray for our troubled youth, who often are what they are because their elders have not been what they should be. Pray that those responsible will make true amends. Lord, have mercy.

Chapter 9

A Word to Organized Groups

Dear Parents,

I have had many interesting experiences during this past year, having completed nearly thirty thousand miles of lecturing and visiting our various field houses of Madonna House. Among the audiences I addressed were many organized groups of Catholic parents who come together in small, cell-like groups to clarify their faith, their vocations, the role of parents and children, and their responsibilities. These groups of Catholic families are vital and courageous!

Yet, I felt a little uneasy. Perhaps because they were uneasy. There was a deep searching of consciences going on among these parents. Much had been clarified. Tremendous achievements could be chalked up to their general credit, yet voices were raised that spoke of dealing only with the periphery. Some parents wanted to take stock and go deeper. Others expressed a strange disquiet because meetings and organization work took them *away from their families*. While they were discussing the family in general, they were neglecting their own. It came to me that perhaps these were the first signs of a malady common to all newer lay apostolates, and dangerous to them as well as to the better-established groups. Other Catholic family and youth groups I encountered were asking much the same questions. It all stemmed from two central points—spiritual training and adequate training for a given apostolate.

There is a grave danger in launching lay apostolates, whatever their goal or aim, without first giving the leaders, and then the rank and file, a profound spiritual formation. This must be done by priests who are well trained in all aspects of the lay apostolate, especially by the appointed chaplains of such groups.

Unless spiritual formation is truly the foundation of any lay apostolate, it will fail. Oh, it may grow like a wild weed for a while. There may be endless meetings, conferences, and conventions. Numbers may, for a while, increase extraordinarily, but it will all add up to something shallow, noisy, and temporary, like froth on beer, or curdled cream in coffee. This is especially applicable to any Catholic lay group dealing with the family, for the family is the vital unit of all society. It sets the tone to any given nation, being its primary root.

Marriage is a *vocation*. That may seem like a trite remark, but it is one that needs repetition. In an old popular lay concept, the vocations of monks, nuns, priests, and brothers were ranked far ahead of the married vocation. Marriage was conceived as something much easier than, say, a Trappist vocation. Yet *every* vocation is a *vocation to love*. All vocations follow the royal road to Christ, with different baggage carriers, to be sure, but there are not five spiritualities in the Catholic Church, or two—the lay and the religious. There is only one, indivisible spirituality. The Ten Commandments are for all. So are the Beatitudes and the evangelical counsels of perfection—poverty, chastity, and obedience. The depth and height of application of these may differ, but there is nothing in the Gospel which says that married folks, according to their vocation, cannot be canonized for poverty, chastity, and obedience, as well as the charitable practices of their state in life. I'll talk more about this in Part 2 of this book.

There seems to be confusion about this in lay minds. There is more confusion about different paths of spiritual formation. Yet they are the same. All Christians are called to a life of prayer: vocal, mental, contemplative, and liturgical. That these will be implemented in different ways and have a different pitch, both inner and outer, does not mean that there is in the Catholic Church a lay spiritual formation of prayer life and a religious formation. No, there is one Catholic formation for both! The proofs of this can be found in the lives of married saints, many of whom were great contemplatives while true to their vocation and state in life.

Human hearts are hungry for roots of ideas and concepts. They want to know where to start. And inevitably, when someone arises honestly, in search of God, it is then that God leads them to the root of all things—his divine Son, our Lord Christ.

Then they begin to see the true foundation of any action done for the Lord. Then they catch a glimpse of *being* for the Lord, before *doing* for him. Then they begin the inward journey everyone must begin in order to meet the God who dwells within the soul.

Husbands and wives gathered together with others like them will have to undertake this inward journey, each person alone and then each couple together. Afterward they will need to share their findings with other couples. They will find, as they journey inward, that action begins by clearing all things that impede the growth of roots. Much has to be weeded, destroyed, reshaped.

The vocation to love, in fact each vocation, demands death to self, the utter forgetting of the pronoun "I." It demands a selflessness that blends with God's. This will lead to a regular prayer life. And it will lead to further depths—the realization that all vocations are hard, as hard as the Cross of Christ, made of green, unplaned wood.

Next will come their painful entry into Christ's passion—his crucifixion and lifting up—and then joy and peace, and the beginning of true action. This is not action for action's sake. It is the fruit of a love that has died to self, of a soul free from earthly attachments and, hence, able to love as God loves. It is love ready to begin to serve, as love must serve—without counting the cost.

Unless all lay apostolates clarify these fundamental principles of a lasting foundation that will result in a great fecundity, they will become confused and inwardly upset, and will die without knowing that they did so.

Part 2

Cana Conversations

One of Madonna House's programs is a summer retreat for families called Cana Colony, an outreach which Catherine established in 1952. Every July and August, families from many places come to Cana for a week of combined family vacation and retreat. Several families are received each week.

Cana is located a short distance from Madonna House, in a wooded area near a lake. The main purpose of Cana Colony is to help families share their lives in Christian community, and to find strength in Christ to live out their vocation. (See also page xi.)

For many years, Catherine spoke to the parents who came to Cana Colony. Many excerpts from Catherine's talks to parents are included here, as well as various questions addressed to her by parents, along with her answers. These frank, sometimes free-wheeling discussions took place in the 1970s and early 1980s, but the issues are still pertinent today, as parents continue to deal with the influence of the media, exercise discipline to teach their children obedience, strive to rise to the challenges facing their teenagers, learn to pray, and struggle to live as Christian families in an increasingly materialistic and atheistic culture.

Let's join Catherine now, on a warm summer afternoon, where she's gathered outside with a group of parents under the shade of a tree near the lake.

Chapter 10

Searching for God

So, here you are, a group of parents with children of various ages from babies to teenagers, in a world that is inimical to the very existence of Christianity. When I look at families like you, and all that you're up against, I know it requires a fantastic amount of prayer to buck the tide all around you. I don't know anything today outside of prayer that can, in a manner of speaking, save the family. You are up against everything, and all at once.

The Church knows what you are up against. I remember when I had a private audience with Pope Pius XII, he said to me, "Madam, no matter what happens to your apostolate, the Father of Christendom implores you to look after families in the best way you can, because they are the future of the Church. The Church is going to be in a great upheaval very soon, and, most of all, the family will suffer." Of course, we all thought that Pope Pius XII was sort of a prophetic man, and he proved to be.

My heart goes out to you, because I, too, have a son and I've been married twice. Both my husbands are dead, God rest their souls, and now my son is old enough to have his own children. And here you are, young enough to have both older children and younger children.

A sort of compassion envelopes me when I think of your young ones. I wish that the world were a better place for them to live in. I wish that we would change our lifestyle, become more Christian, stop being concerned for ourselves, and become concerned with others.

All those things I wish, and I think that's what you wish too, but that means changing the whole system of government, of life, of everything. Is it possible? Yes, all things are possible —in God. I know that, because I've seen what God can do.

I've seen a lot here at Madonna House. So many people come here. This year alone, there will be close to eight thousand who will pass through Madonna House—most of them young people of 20, 21, 22, or 23 years of age. They will come from California, from Florida, from British Columbia, the Yukon, from all over—Germany, France, Portugal, Brazil. Why do they come to Madonna House?

If you ask them directly, they say they come in search of God. But that's impossible, because their parents should have given them God! What are parents for? To give their children God! But maybe they haven't done that, because the kids come here in search of him. (I speak very frankly to you who are parents. I hope you don't mind.)

Now these young people, when they come to us, are frightened and searching. There is one boy who just arrived two days ago. His name is Carlos, a Spanish boy from New Jersey, about eighteen or nineteen, tall and thin. He walked up to me today and said, "You know something? I've found what I was looking for." I said, "You have?" He said, "Yes. Love." I said, "Well, that's mighty fine. In two days you found love." He said, "The funny part is that *all* of you people love me. It's not just one person. It's all of you who love me. This is terrific. This is wonderful. This is what I was looking for. A place where people love one another." Well! That's fine, but loving one another is a perfectly normal state of Christian affairs. Isn't it? Shouldn't he find love wherever there are Christians?

Anyway, they come, these young people, by the hundreds every year. They come seeking not only God and love, but the beatitudes of Jesus Christ, beatitudes like "Blessed are the poor, for they shall inherit the earth" (Mt 5:3).

They are not all poor, these kids. I looked at one boy and I said, "Your face is familiar to me." And he said, "Yes. You probably saw me with my father." Then I remembered his father is a big shot in Toronto. This boy said, "We have a live-in maid, a live-in cook, a live-in butler. So that should go to show you who we are. That's why I left home. I couldn't stand it. I was up to my neck in all that stuff."

You see, our children don't understand the strange situation of wealth and poverty existing side by side. We cannot go on with this. To *share* is what God meant us to do.

Be careful to give away whatever you can give away voluntarily, because poverty is all around you. You don't have to go any place to find poverty. There is poverty right here. Wherever you come from, New York, Chicago or a back-bush country, it makes no difference. There are pockets of poverty everywhere.

Now, strangely enough, in the midst of all of this, there comes a figure. Do you have a vivid imagination? There is a figure called Lady Poverty and you look at her and you say, "Yes." Once upon a time, she attracted me very much, but that was so long ago I can't remember. Well, it's time to be attracted to Lady Poverty again. Now is the time. We have to change, because catastrophic conditions are so close to us that if we don't change, we will be caught like little insects on a needle.

You may be thinking how can I say this? You have to understand that I have seen so much. I've been through World War I and the Russian Revolution. I experienced the horror of the Spanish Civil War. I was in Germany just before Hitler took over and in Warsaw when the Germans invaded. So you see, you have before you a witness to what can happen in this world. I saw Germans pay one million marks for one loaf of bread when inflation soared. I saw inflation die, and then there was no money to sell any more. After the Revolution in Russia, I dropped to a weight of eighty-two pounds. I was so hungry I ate rats and mice and anything that you can possibly find to eat. I chewed on wood just to have something in my mouth.

So out of the depths of all this experience, I want to help you to see, because I love you. And I tell you this: Be watchful. Be watchful before the Lord. Listen to what he says. Stop thinking of yourself and start thinking about God. Get together and think about how to bring God to people, so that your children and other children can live in peace.

You live in a rich nation, as nations go. Many of you live in Canada or the U.S., so, compared to much of the world, you live in wealth. This is the time in which you will have to give up an awful lot, unless some other groups take it away from you.

As some of you may know, my husband and I fled the Russian Revolution. We were wealthy but we dressed as peasants, otherwise the communists would have arrested us. After they went through our apartment, we had nothing left, though we had owned a lot. My husband's father was a millionaire and we had maids and all that sort of stuff. My friends, it took them just three days to smash the whole thing up. We were ordered to bring the key to our safety deposit box and come to the bank. There we were put in line, and everything in the deposit box—stocks, bonds, money, jewelry, whatever —they put in big bags and went away with it. I had jewelry of the de Huecks that had been handed down for generations. They took it all, just like that, without any problems. Eleven centuries of goods departed—whoosh! Then they came to our apartment and took away everything—even the mattress! We slept on the floor, my husband and I.

Perhaps this is what's in store for you. Politically, will we hold onto capitalism so tightly that we're going to have yet another Hitler or Stalin? What is going to happen?

I wish I could tell you something that would be cheerful, but there *is* something cheerful, because if you're in love with God, pain becomes joy. And then all things are easy because they're all done for God and with God. But we are afraid of pain. We're afraid because we don't have faith. But remember, pain is the kiss of Christ. And there is no love without pain.

If you're in love with a guy and he's driving to Chicago and it's raining, you worry that he'll skid and be hurt. There are thousands of people going to Chicago, but you're not worried about them. You're worried about the one you love. Where there is love, there is worry and there is pain.

We have to change. We have to stop being afraid of pain and have faith. We have to love and not be afraid to change the way we live for fear it will cause us pain. Christ said, "Blessed are the poor, for they shall inherit the earth." We will, if we are poor.

So if you decide that it's time to change the way you live; don't be afraid. He will be right there with you, helping you. That's all he's waiting for, that Christians should become Christian. Then we will be able to go to a big New York or Toronto or wherever—and say, "Oh, look how those Christians love one another." Their love will be evident. It will stand out for all to see. Can we say that now?

Christ is waiting for us to decide. Listen. Hear his voice? He says, "This is the hour! Listen! Listen, my people. This is the hour. Tomorrow will be too late. All I ask is a change of heart. All I ask is that you pass the Good News on to someone else. All I ask is that the Good News be heard. And the only Good News left to hear is that I love you. I have given my life for you. And now it is your turn. It's your turn. If you want peace tomorrow, incarnate my covenant today."

There are so many who have yet to hear the Good News. Many are young people. One girl who is twenty came to me and said, "Who is that man, Jesus Christ, that you're talking about all the time?" I said, "You don't know about him?" She said "No. My family is into transcendental meditation. They never talk about God." She's twenty years old and she doesn't know who Jesus Christ is! Isn't that enough to make you feel sad?

So, anyway, we see these children, these young people between the ages of eighteen and twenty-five or so. They come to Madonna House restless and unhappy. They are searching. They say, "We're looking for God," as if they were looking with a magnifying glass. And do you know what they want? They want proof that we live the Gospel without compromise, or try to. They want to see it lived. They want to touch it to be sure it's real. They want to touch me, and our staff, and it takes them quite a while to believe. But then they say, "Yes. It's true. You practice the Gospel without compromise, or try to."

That reminds me of my mother. When I was about six, I was interested in Jesus Christ, so I said, "Mummy, I'd like to touch God." My mother said, "Touch me." That was a very theological question and answer, only I didn't realize it then. She and Christ were the same. Christ said, "Whatsoever you do to the least of my brothers, you do to me" (Mt 25:40).

The kids who come to Madonna House want to see the Gospel lived. They want to see God and they want to touch him. And when they don't touch God at home, they go elsewhere searching for him and sometimes they end up here with us. Eventually, when their story comes out, it's about mama and papa. Maybe your kids are here, I don't know. We don't ask them personal questions about who they are and so forth, but because you mean so much to them, they are preoccupied with you. You may not think so, because they look nonchalant and run away, but it isn't so. They care about you and what you do—or what you don't do.

I was talking to one boy at the table the other day. We never ask our guests what their family does or any questions like that. So he said, "Do you know who I am?" I said, "No." He said, "I'm a day-care baby." I said, "A what?" He said, "I'm a day-care baby. My mother deposited me in day-care when I was a very little baby. Then I was sent to a baby-care center during the summer. I was sent to boarding school for grade school and during the summer I was sent to summer camp. Then I was sent away to boarding school for high school. Now I'm eighteen and I'm tired of being boarded out and so I ran away. That's why I'm here."

I tried to explain to him that it's not exactly a sin to send a child to boarding school, but then he looked at me and he said, "No, there is no sin, but when you're a little shaver and you come home, there is no peanut butter sandwich made by Mama; it's always done by a maid." Now how can you reconcile that?

So now, I say to you young mothers, you had better start being homemakers. Because this kind of thing just can't go on. It can't.

There was so much pain in the eyes of that boy he was like a battered child. I couldn't stand looking at him very much. He said to me, "My mother is always working. If she needed to work, I would understand, but she doesn't. We have a big, beautiful house, a very nice one. We have a maid and a live-in cook. No, she doesn't need to work, but she wants another car, another TV, another dress, and she is for women's lib. She wants to be somebody. It's not enough for her to be a mother."

That boy is still at Madonna House, looking for a mother. I can be a substitute mother for him and he can weep on my shoulder, but I'm not his mother. What's his real mother doing? She's busy in California, doing something; I don't know what. We located her. We told her where her son was. Since he ran away we thought she would be worried and so forth. She just said, "I'm so happy he's at Madonna House." Period. That ended the conversation. It's not like that with everybody, but there are too many kids like that, and they come to us here at Madonna House. They are seeking love. They are seeking poverty, simplicity. In other words, seeking God, because God is love, God is simple, God is poor.

What we need is a change in society, according to the Christian ideal. Christ gave us a new commandment. He said, "Love one another as I have loved you." (Jn 13:34) Have you honestly, truthfully, adhered to that commandment? God asks us to love as Christ himself loved, as God loved.

We have that power, to love as God loved. Do we do that? Is it visible? Can we go around Toronto, New York, or Chicago and see Christians and say, "Look at how those Christians love one another"? Can we? No. So, what's happened? What's gone wrong? Tell me. It's more appropriate that you should tell me instead of my telling you, because I have all these young people who come here to Madonna House, and they come here looking for love.

How are you going to do it? How are you going to love? There's only one answer. With God, there is only one answer. And that answer is prayer.

Chapter 11

Learning about Prayer

Now I want to tell you about prayer. I have written books on prayer, but really it is, ultimately, a mystery. You can't just grab it and hold it, but let me see if I can tell you a little bit about prayer.

First, let me repeat that I have been married. I mention this fact because I think it entitles me to know how to pray, for the simple reason that it teaches me to know how to love, and I think that prayer is love.

Now, you have to approach the situation of prayer sensibly. It's not vocal prayer only. Sure, it begins with that. First there's the "Hail Mary, full of grace" and all those prayers you learned when you were a child. In the beginning, we are naturally inclined to talk to God out loud, which is vocal prayer. When we are very young we like Santa Claus. We want a red carriage. Then we get older and we begin to meditate.

A good way to understand meditation, for you who are married, is like this. First, think back to the time before you met your spouse. Picture it now. Here you are—you're single and unattached and happy, and one day, you go to a dance. And there you meet a boy and you enjoy the dance, and he walks you home from the dance, and you're smitten—*Zap! Zam!* He's a nice guy, see, and suddenly, you've lost your heart. So you're at home. You're lying in bed and you think of all he said to you and how nice that he asked you to dinner three days from now.

Now, you men, think about when you first fell in love with your wife, but before you were married. Wasn't she always on your mind? Wasn't the face of your beloved always before you? It was. I know it was, because it was with me and it was with a lot of other people who got married.

When I worked in a hospital, we used to have a nurse who would sing, "I love Georgie, I love Georgie." Georgie was her boyfriend and he was in the men's ward. And she used to sing, "I love Georgie" and she would swivel around with a bed pan to the tune of "I love Georgie." I said to her, "Look, one of these days, you're going to spill that thing." But she would just swivel around some more and sing, "I love Georgie; I love Georgie." Well, if you can do that when you have a bedpan in your hand, evidently you can do it with other things too.

But to be in love with God! Just think of it! To be in love with God. Think for a moment what it means to be in love with God, to have him always before your face. It happens to you as you pray ordinary prayers. Suddenly, you hunger for a closer relationship with God. You begin to meditate on what he said. You read the Gospel. You read his words and you say to yourself, "I read that a long time ago. Why didn't I understand?"

When you are courting, or when you're engaged to someone, what do you think about? You think about what he or she said to you. You meditate on it. You savor the words of your beloved. Meditation is like that. So when we enter into the prayer of meditation, the words of God that the Holy Spirit illuminates hit you. You say to yourself, "Oh! I have seen that word, seen that sentence many times. Why haven't I understood it before now?" Well, there is a time for everything. There is a time for understanding.

Then, slowly, very slowly, the prayer changes to contemplation. I don't mean that it necessarily has to, but it may. What is contemplation? It's very simple for married people to understand. It's like the time when you are married and you live together as man and wife and there is that ecstatic moment when you achieve your marital act. At the end of this moment, when you're lying in the arms of your husband and he in yours, you contemplate each other. You don't talk, because it is so beautiful and so powerful. This is not the time for conversation. It's the time for listening to each other's heart. You lie in the arms of your husband or your wife and you are absolutely silent.

It is the same with the prayer of contemplation. There comes a time when words are cheap. They sound hollow. They don't answer anything. So you just look at Christ and he looks at you, as if you were a husband or a wife. For, after all, you are a member of his Church and he is the Bridegroom of the Church. You remain there by his side and you look at him. And he looks at you. You have met something. You have met Someone. Now you're consummated. Now you don't have to read any spiritual books. You don't need to read anything. It's not a time for talking. It's a time for listening to God's heart. So you enter into the prayer of contemplation by the simple fact that you begin to think of God directly.

Then, eventually, he speaks; not to everyone, but to the listener. You have to listen. You have to listen very carefully because the footsteps of God are very soft, like a whisper. The Lord used to come to talk to Adam and Eve in the twilight. And they never knew when he was coming, because they couldn't hear his footsteps.

Slowly, very slowly, you begin to hear. You hear the same thing that you read before, but now it comes from the innermost part of your heart. Now you know that it's the Omega who speaks and you know what contemplative prayer is like.

Then to some of you, God gives a key, and with it, you enter a void. It is a void where everything is suddenly whole and you yourself suddenly become whole. You're not fragmented any more. In that strange void, there is the heart of God, to which he has given you the key. You become whole and everything looks clear and now you don't ask questions any more, because there is no need for questions. You know exactly what you have to do, because he tells you. The Holy Spirit tells you. Do you remember what Christ said about the Holy Spirit? He said, "I will leave you an Advocate who will remind you of what I taught you" (Jn 14:26). If we have to be reminded, the Advocate is the reminder in that absolute void where we are whole.

Then, you see, nothing matters any more. Then a person like yourself is quite able to endure every obnoxious detail of the neighbors, the irritations of your children and your spouse and everyday life.

But you must have faith. The difficulty is faith. You don't enter the void unless you have faith. And because your education from childhood in America and Canada is one of the head, you want to sift everything through your head before you understand. But theology is a science about God, and there is only one Person who can teach us that science—God himself.

I took Thomistic theology and never used it. St. Thomas Aquinas said that after he once saw Christ, he wanted to burn the whole *Summa*, his momentous theological work. I remember when I was studying Thomistic theology, I said to my teacher, "Why are we studying this? Fundamentally, it's all charity, right? Why don't we just dip into Christ with his charity?" Well, the teacher was a good and holy priest who was also my spiritual director at the time, and he wanted me to study theology, so I did.

Really theology is very simple. You lie flat on your stomach. Go to sleep if you wish. Suddenly, you open the Bible and it's as if a light goes on and you say, "My God, I read and re-read that word, that sentence for ages, but now it's all new." Someone is teaching you, but it's not your teacher. It's God.

So, you learn prayer and the various means of prayer. All the ways of prayer can sometimes go together. Sometimes I sit there and I say, "Lord, look. I think I've had enough. I think this lay apostolate is for the birds. Why don't you skip it for a while? I'm fed up—to here." Maybe you feel the same way about marriage some days too. But usually after I say that, he answers in my heart, "So was I fed up to here, but I died for you; now you die for me." How can you answer that one?

I have this bad knee. I got it while I was in the Holy Land, of all places. I went three steps down an Arab stairway and injured it. I said to God, "Is that nice? I come to visit you and you allow me to hurt my knee. Look, I've practically got to go to the Mayo Clinic to have that knee fixed." Anyway, do you know what he said to me? "I fell for you, and now you fall for me." So I fell for him all right. I fell for him like a ton of bricks. And he fell for me like two tons of bricks. So I never complain about my bad knee any more.

Now, as you pray, eventually, one day, you *become* a prayer. Gone are all the vocal prayers, the meditation, and contemplation. It's just that you have become a prayer in yourself. You are at the feet of God and you don't have to ask for anything, because he knows all that you need. In the immense silence and solitude that exists between you and God, all things come forth.

There is no meditation, no contemplation. No kind of prayer at all. Because *you* become a prayer. When you believe, really believe, totally and completely, you *become* the Gospel. When you become the Gospel and enter into the void, you can change the world.

Still you have to experience something else. You have to experience the kiss of Christ. It is said in the Old Testament, in the Song of Solomon, "He kissed me with the kiss of his mouth" (Sng 1:2). There is another saying too: Pain is the kiss of Christ.

Love and pain walk side by side. All your life, that is a fact. When you love someone, and he has taken a trip in a car or on a plane, you are afraid of a crash. Where there is love, there is worry and pain. We have to experience that pain in order to understand what prayer is, what the preaching of the Gospel is. Without pain, we can't do it.

You know, it is necessary to pray to be a good parent, to bring your child up to his full maturity so that he, too, can pray and can turn into a prayer. That is the duty of the parents. Prayer is vitally important in order to do it.

Prayer appears to many people to be very unimportant in the whole scheme of things, in the midst of the mess of life. But only prayer can gird you with faith. Pray for faith—strong faith. You must be totally directed by a faith that nothing can shake, neither persecution nor martyrdom nor anything else. So pray for a faith that is total, strong, and straight as an arrow. As you become a prayer within, your faith will move you upward to God. Nothing will disturb you. As St. Teresa of Avila said, "Let nothing disturb you." Things that would normally disrupt you won't, because you will have faith.

Now, listen carefully. Here's what I'm trying to say: Even when it has seemed impossible to raise your children in the totality of faith, if you become a prayer, and if you and your spouse together become a prayer also, then even in the midst of chaos, you will find it is possible to raise your children. It is in the midst of this chaos now—not tomorrow, not the day after, but now—that we have to stand straight in total faith and accept a new style of living, in which prayer and poverty—sharing our goods with others—take precedence over a lot of things. When we do that, then something is going to happen to the children. Then they will see what they come here to Madonna House to find. They will see the Gospel lived without compromise, and they won't have to go any further than you to find love and God, because they will see it in you, and they will see it in their own home.

Media Influence

Question: One of the big problems that married couples and families are facing today is the influence of the media on their children: television, radio, movies, everything. And the children's heroes are not the heroes we'd like them to have. What do you have to say about this?

Answer: Do you have to have a television? The unsavory heroes will disappear if you don't have one. You see, television is a baby-sitter. It gives you time, but television is not a very good thing for a child at this point. Now, when you take, for instance, "The Incredible Hulk" and such shows, that's horrible stuff. The kids wake up in the night and yell from watching it. So there comes a time when you've got to stop it. You have the power to stop it very simply, by turning it off, and also by not buying the product of the company that sponsors it.

Another thing is to go to the program sponsors and make them do something about objectionable programs. Go to those people who pay for the show and tell them that you want that program off—and it's off. If there are enough of you, they'll do something. There are groups that are fighting television, in fact the Sears Roebuck Company recently took off a show it sponsored because it wasn't the kind of show that should be around.

Comment: But their peers, the other kids at school, are always talking about their heroes. Do you feel that maybe just prayer would help?

Answer: Well, it could be enough, if you teach them well. Let me give you an example by talking about my parents. My mother used to like to eat salted herring. When we were in Switzerland my mother sent me out to buy salted herring from a little shop. The herrings' heads and tails came off and the whole thing was a salty mess. So the kids I met on the way home made fun of me and said, "Pooh, pooh, pooh, pooh. Look at her—she hasn't got money to buy anything but those salted herring." You know how kids are.

With tears in my eyes I took the thing to my mother and she said to me, "Do you mean to say you are in tears about that? Here's another ten cents. Go and buy another herring." I said, "But the kids are going to laugh at me." She said, "Okay. Stand up and be laughed at. Tell them about Jesus Christ. Tell them that Jesus Christ could not afford much because he didn't have much money, so he would get a salted herring. Go ahead and do it." I was about seven years old at the time, and I said, "Okay, I'll do it."

I stood with that messy thing dripping down, that salted herring, and I pushed it all around, and the kids were watching and laughing. I said, "You dumb clucks don't know nothing from nothing. Jesus Christ would have eaten that herring and been happy with it. What's the matter with being poor? Christ was poor!" Well, in two minutes, the kids disappeared. That was my first lecture. So, I came back with the herring to my mother. She said, "Did you tell them?" and I said, "Yes I did, and they all went away."

So you see, it's very simple. Try that on your own children. Say to them, "Do you want to be just a rubber stamp? Do you always want to conform to what everybody says, or do you want to stand up and be counted? Which is it going to be? Why don't you get after those characters, those other kids, and say to them, 'To hell with that junk that you're getting on TV.'" Well, when they hear you say "to hell," they'll listen, because Mama doesn't say "to hell" too often.

Put some backbone into yourself and into them, and tell them to go ahead and really fight. Let's put some backbone into our children. Are they going to get up and fight? Are they going to do something? Or are they going to just sit back and relax? That's the $64,000 question!

When you want to change a lifestyle, it's got to go all the way, because that means changing the nation. And don't kid yourself. It isn't easy, but children, when they believe in something, act on it. They really do. It's going to cost a lot of tears. There won't be TV. You will hear, "But everybody does it, Mom." Oh, that's what they try to tell me. "Everybody does it." I say, "So, you want to be like everybody? Absolutely no difference? Just a rubber stamp? Nothing at all?"

If we want to follow Jesus Christ, we're going to be radical. You know what radical is? The word radical comes from *radix*, which means "root," someone who's rooted deep. In this case, someone who's rooted in the heart of Christ.

Lifestyle Options

Question: A thing that really concerns me relates to more than TV. It relates to society in general. Let me put it this way: If you feel TV is a bad influence, you have the option of getting rid of it or choosing which parts of it you're going to use. Now, with society in general, if you think living in a city is a bad influence on your family, you have the option of seeking ways to deal with the detrimental influence of that environment, or you may decide you don't want to be there at all and go live in the country to get away from it. Is that all of your options and are those legitimate options?

Answer: It depends. If you're single, you can do anything you want since nobody depends on you, but if you have a family, what are you going to do with them? What are your options? You can take them to the boondocks, let's say, and have a very little house and a farm and so forth. There is nothing wrong with that, but everything has to be figured out according to the needs of them all. You see, the word *I* seldom exists in Christianity. The words *they, he,* and *she* do exist. So the first question is, what are the needs of the others?

For example, there is a man I know who desires very much to give up everything and preach the Gospel. This requires thought. He hasn't that many options because he and his wife have children, but he does have certain ones and these are the ones he should discuss with a spiritual director—which way to go. For instance, he limits his TV to the news and certain well-chosen programs for the children. That's the end of television as far as he's concerned. But as for where they live, he's a lawyer and has a very big practice. So, what to do? Depending on your circumstances, your options may be more or less limited.

Comment: I guess one of the aspects of that question is my sense of responsibility. For example, if I have certain talents that I know can help people in a town or a city, I can stay and be of assistance to that community. Yet there are influences and specific things that I want in my quality of life for my family.

Answer: The point is changing your lifestyle. That goes deep, very deep. It goes so deep that it's frightening. It means you have to drop a lot of things. It means you change how you live. You have to share with others whatever is a service in your part of the world.

It's not so much the TV question or even where you're going to live, for tomorrow you might not have a job no matter where you are. I know a fellow who has two Ph.D.s and who worked for NASA—now he's driving a taxi. So where does it all begin? Where does it all end? I think prayer is the first resort and the last resort. Prayer is starting to try to have a lifestyle that is beyond the reach of anybody.

Communities for Families

Question: If parents are trying to raise their children the best way they can, wouldn't it be good if they joined together into some kind of community? We were talking last night about community and how Christian people can really support one another by living their lives together. There seems to be a real need for this because we don't have a Christian world any more. Are you in favor of families forming communities?

Answer: No. Many parents are thinking about it as you are. They say they need a community because the world today is such a mess. Well, I agree that the world is a mess, but people who have tried to make communities of families have had great difficulty. We tried, for instance, to make a community of married people and it didn't succeed at all. They quarreled among themselves. Dorothy Day tried to do the same thing shortly before we did. She had the same experience.

How shall I explain it? I've seen some of those communities on my lecture trips. In one case, one of the boys from a family in a community got older and went to college. He wanted to live in the dormitory but the family couldn't afford it, so they wanted to get the money from the community. Well, it ended in a mess. It's very difficult.

One community has single men and women, priests and married people. It doesn't work. For a while, yes. But not for long. Let's say you are two married people and you have children, okay? Suppose you always have a single person living with you, always around. What for? They interfere with your life. The single should go with the single and the married with the married.

And I would never suggest that married couples live together in a house, sharing their meals and so forth. Let me give you a picture. Let's say that one girl's name is Becky and the other is Jean. Becky and Jean and their husbands decide to live together in one house with all their children—all together in amenity and holiness and stuff. I come to visit and say hello. Already, opening the door, I hear a terrible noise. It's Becky telling Jean: "I don't want your brat to come and do anything to mine. She's my child and I don't want you ..." This is a true picture, isn't it? The average person can uphold that sort of thing for about three months, but it won't last. I try to tell people it doesn't work, but they always try.

Personally, as a married woman, I would never join a community. We Russians don't go in for this joining business. Communities and all the rest is not our forte. We have a natural community life with father, mother, children, aunt, uncle and so forth. But this joining business, no thank you. I've been married myself. I have a son. When I was young and my child was small, why would I have joined a community? I had the community of the Trinity. In my matrimonial venture, I walked up the three steps of an altar and I was married. And by being married, I joined the Father, Son and Holy Spirit. So we're all one community—those Three and me and my husband, and later the baby. Why should I join a community? I am myself the master of my mystery under the Trinity. I don't need a community. Boris and I, Eddie and I did not need help from anyone for the simple reason that we were whole—one husband and wife—connected with the Trinity. Why do we need to have a bunch of people around us? I don't want somebody else raising my child.

I have not recommended communities for families. You see, there exist so few communities of any kind which really work. I think they can only work if they have poverty, chastity and obedience, and no married people. Look at me. Eddie and I were married and we ended up unmarried, so to speak, for the sake of the community of Madonna House.

Comment: You didn't set out to join a community—the community joined you.

Answer: That's true. When I began, my apostolate was a lone one. I went by myself to the poor in Toronto. I was alone. I had a little eight-quart basket and I begged for what I needed. Suddenly, out of the blue, three girls and two boys come to me and they said, "Catherine, we want to join you." I said, "Oh, no. We Russians don't go in for this joining business. You go and join nuns and priests and all that sort of stuff; communities and all the rest is not our forte." So, off they went.

Three weeks later, the secretary of the Archbishop said, "His Excellency wants to see you." I said, "Oh, oh." He said, "Catherine, why don't you want to take those characters?" I said, "Very simply, I have an eight-quart basket ..." and I went through the whole rigmarole. "Well," he said, "all you have to do is get an eleven-quart basket." He had a sense of humor, this archbishop. He said, "Money will come if you have faith." So I had faith. And that's how you happen to be here.

There is one kind of community for families that works, and it's very good. Slowly, families living in the same town gather into one parish. They rent or buy houses or apartments for themselves so each family lives alone with its own children. About three times a week and especially on Sunday, they come together. They have picnics and so forth. And they have a spiritual director who keeps them together. You understand what I mean. It does not work when you live together.

One thing though—you will not form a community of any kind if you are selfish. You have to be unselfish. You must accept the motto that we have at Madonna House: "I am third."

God is first; my neighbor is second. I am third. It's difficult, because in the course of making a community, you have to subdue an awful lot of American and Canadian ideas—the individualistic stuff. Americans and Canadians are very individualistic. It is very difficult for the community with individualistic members in it.

Teenagers Going Steady

Question: What do you think of teenagers between the ages of fifteen and eighteen going steady? Do you think it should be allowed?

Answer: No. Let me explain why. The teen years are the time of swift physical maturing, but not of emotional maturity. Emotionally, whether they know it or not, teenagers are yet children. While their bodies may seem to be those of fully developed men and women, they act as they should emotionally—as children reaching out toward maturity, but as yet far from achieving it.

One of the signs of maturity is the ability to take responsibility. At some distant and past time, when the marriage age was much younger, young people did not need to exercise this sense of responsibility. In an agricultural culture, they remained under parental roofs, and went on with the familiar work of the farm or cattle ranch, adding to the general security of the whole family by adding one more person to contribute to the work thereof. Today such a life, secure and simple, under a parental roof, would be unthinkable. Moreover, the very swift current of modern life, the highly competitive stream of it, and the need for ever wider and more specialized education and skills, retard perforce, the marriageable age.

Hence, going steady, which implies definite selection of a life partner, is deadly. Neither party is truly ready to make that choice. Both the boy and the girl lack the vision and the yardsticks for making this selection for life. Moreover, going steady in today's modern way of life, to mince no words, is definitely an occasion of sin to both. It is quite obvious to anyone with an ounce of common sense that fifteen is much too early to even think of marriage. And under fifteen —preposterous! I was married for the first time at fifteen myself. I know what I'm talking about!

Here is where parental authority must be exercised to the full. For when viewed from a mature point of view, "going steady" in the teen years borders on the ridiculous. My answer is a plain, simple *No*.

In my travels I have noticed that parents have a preoccupation with teenagers going steady and the matter of sexuality. These seem to be two of the most worrisome questions of the day. They want to know how to teach the vital truths of life to their children and how to make children and youth understand the infinite beauty, holiness and divine purpose of sexuality. The only answer is to make your home what it should be—a novitiate for your children for the sublime vocation, future married life! The answer begins almost in the cradle. We must restore the home to Christ.

Chapter 12

The Duty of the Moment

Today another group of parents is gathering at Cana Colony to hear Catherine speak. This time, it is a diverse group of families from many different places. Let's join them now.

I understand that you come from all parts of the world, yet, fundamentally, you are all the same. You are all parents; you all have families. Yet what really binds us together is what binds us to the Lord—our love for him.

There is another thing you have in common, and that is something deep within you that is not getting an outlet because of the secularism of the society that surrounds us, because of atheism. I'm not talking about communistic atheism, I'm talking of simple apathy, a disregard for God, even a non-belief in God. It hits you hard. I know it hits me hard. We live and move in a sea of apathy, of selfishness, of greed, and we say to ourselves, "But I am baptized—something has got to be different for me. This is not the kind of life that I really want to lead."

The difficult situation for Christians is that the world has become more and more secular. Years ago there were no hijackings, no terrorist bombings. What's happened? Not too long ago I was at Dulles Airport in Washington, D.C., sitting there, waiting for a plane. The lady next to me was shaking like a leaf. I am a nurse, and so I said to her, "Can I be of any assistance to you, Madam?" She said, "I just came off a

hijacking. I was going to Boston and they took us to Timbuktu."
So, we don't know these days where we are going, not only in
the sense of that lady who thought she was going to Boston
from Washington and who landed in Timbuktu. We simply
don't know where we are going in life. We're at sixes and
sevens over this most tragic situation, and we're not alone.

If we were single people, it wouldn't matter so much, but
here you are, you have children. Look at this little one
here—he's an absolutely perfect little child, and what kind of a
world are we making for him? Is it his ultimate destiny to die of
an exploded bomb? Or to just go begging like a hobo? What
will it be? We have to face up to the fact that this little fellow
here is going to grow up and be a big fellow like you. It's worth
laying down your life for this child. So this is the time to
reappraise our values and to change the way we live our lives.
We have to do something that will make a safe place for him.
And his safety depends on our lifestyle.

Let's face it: we have to look at our life and change our
lifestyle. We Christians have to stop wanting so many material
things. We have to stop worshipping things and we have to start
loving. We have to love as Christ loves. Do you people come to
New York or Chicago or any town that's around the corner and
clap your hands and say, "Oh, look how those Catholics love
one another." Do you feel that way? Do we love one another
deeply and sincerely? With grave humility and infinite
meekness, in the way of Jesus Christ? Think about it. Do we?

These days there is trouble everywhere. I just returned
from Houston, Texas and at the airport, the man in charge of the
luggage said "Don't go out after 11:30 P.M., because they are
apt to slit your pocket or slit your belly." I said to myself, what
barbarism have we come to? You have to acknowledge we are
in a state of barbarism today, with violence born of anger. It is
a terrible anger, this desire to kill without any reason. It reminds
me of when I was in Russia and the Red soldiers came and held
a husband and a wife. The wife was tiny and very slender and
they threw her from the fifth floor and laughed while they did

it. Now that kind of senseless killing is part of life, and you have to face it because there's an awful lot of anger in America and Canada. We're facing the end of an era, like the Romans, like the Babylonians.

There is only one thing that's going to help us and that is prayer. It's time to turn to God. Nothing else can help us. Don't be afraid. Just begin to pray.

Don't go and say a lot of prayers or anything like that. Just pray in a very simple way, perhaps for the first time in your lives. Maybe for you it's different, but for so many people, God seems very distant. But he's really right there, with you.

I always invite him for a cup of coffee. Do you know that God never drank a cup of coffee in his life while he lived on earth? They had no coffee. Mentally, I invite him for coffee. I take the Bible and put it between us. I say, "Lord, you sit there and I sit here. Here is your cup of coffee and here is my cup of coffee, and we're going to have a dialogue from your own book called the Gospel. So now I'll be the apostles and you be yourself." You'll be surprised what happens when you do that. Just have a simple discussion with God over the Gospel. If I can meditate on the Gospel, so can you, but it changes your whole life when you do. You'll start to look at life differently.

Here's an example of what I mean. Dorothy Day of the Catholic Worker, who will probably be one of the canonized saints of America someday, was lecturing to a group during the Depression of the 1930s and she was saying that the people are so hungry that when they knock at our door we should give them a sandwich or something. One of the ladies said, "Yes, but they can kill you," and Dorothy, who has a perfectly lovely face and whose eyes sparkle, said, "So they can. Isn't it wonderful to be a martyr for Christ's sake?" There was a hush in the whole audience. Everybody shut up because nobody felt like being a martyr but it wouldn't have done for them to have said so.

Dorothy went on. "If he asks for your coat, give him a pair of trousers too—your husband's." A woman objected, "But then my husband won't have a pair of trousers." Dorothy replied,

"Ah, you have very little faith. If you give to the poor, God will supply." So out of the audience, another woman said, "I'll try it." She had a new suit that had belonged to an uncle who had died. The uncle's wife had given her the suit for her husband, who was exactly the same size as the uncle. The woman gave it away, and after that, she got completely converted to the idea of giving to the poor.

So you see, life changes when you start to have faith and live the Gospel. But there is more to all of this, something that is hard to put into words. It is a kind of joy. Do you feel what I feel? When I have a surplus of something, it is such a joy to give it to others.

I learned what a joy it was to serve the poor from my parents. Let me tell you a little story to show what I mean.

When I was growing up in Russia, my father was a diplomat. One time he and my mother gave a big, fancy tea party at our home for several hundred ambassadors and dignitaries. We were in the middle of having formal tea, with everyone using nice china and so forth. I was about nine years old at the time, and I was allowed to be there, all dressed up and carrying little cakes and being polite. Suddenly, the butler opened the door and announced to my father, "Christ is at the door." Well, the French ambassador's wife dropped her expensive tea cup on the rug. She was not used to such interruptions!

Father excused himself, mother excused herself and off they went. And whom did they welcome? A hobo who had come to the door begging. And what did they do? My mother and father served him themselves, even though we had fourteen servants in the house. My mother laid out the best linen, the most expensive silver and our best china and so forth, and she served a hobo. My father did likewise. I saw all of this and I wanted to serve the hobo too, but Mother said, "Oh no. You were not obedient last week; you cannot serve Christ unless you are obedient." So, in my little mind, to serve the poor was a great honor and a great joy.

Now that's Christianity. You don't have to have catechism lessons when you see that sort of thing. That was how my parents treated the poor, so that was what my brother and I learned from growing up in that kind of household, thanks be to God.

Of course, I was like any other kid too. I would say, "Well, do we live in a monastery or something like that?" My parents would say, "No. We live in a family, of which Christ is the head." So, in the end, it all seemed quite natural to me to serve the poor. Christ was in the poor and we must serve him. Later on, it seemed very natural at Friendship House and Madonna House when the poor would come, to see that it was Christ who came, so we treated them accordingly. I learned that from my parents, when I was a child.

The parents' faith penetrates their children by example, you see. Now look at yourselves. Here you are with children of your own. What do your children learn? They learn only whatever you can give them. So I implore you, put your Catholicity on the table for your children to see. Let them see it clearly. Let them read it in big, clear letters. This requires faith—and you get faith by praying for it.

I learned all this from my parents and part of the reason I learned it so well was that I grew up in a Christian environment. But for you today, life is different. You do not have a Christian environment as we had. You have to re-Christianize society, because you are Christians. Re-Christianize it! Change it!

Now how do we do that, the way things are today? We are so busy these days that it's as if we are enmeshed in a merry-go-round or roller coaster. Faster, faster, faster—that's us. And we don't know if we're going forward, backward or which way. Christ said, "I have come to serve" (Mt 20:28), and so should we. Christ said, "Pray always," so we should. Here we are, well indoctrinated in our religion, presumably. But the world goes round about like this all around us—more selfish, more greedy, more horrible than before. Faster, faster, faster it goes. And what should we do? How should we live in this world today?

How should we serve? Well, the answer that I've come to see, after fifty years in this lay apostolate, is to do the duty of the moment.

What Is the Duty of the Moment?

The duty of the moment is what you should be doing at any given time, in whatever place God has put you. You may not have Christ in a hobo at your door, but you may have a little child. If you have a child, your duty of the moment may be to change a dirty diaper. So you do it. But you don't just change that diaper, you change it to the best of your ability, with great love for both God and that child. Do you do it like that? You can see Christ in that child.

Or your duty of the moment may be to scrub your floors. Do you scrub your floors well? With great love for God? If not, do it. If you see to it that your house is well-swept, your food is on the table, and there is peace during the meal, then there is this slow order that is established, and the immense tranquility of God's order falls upon you and your family. Yes, there is order, because while we keep thinking of others,, things get clear in our hearts. Then we can forget ourselves.

The duty of the moment, our nitty-gritty, daily, ordinary routine of life, can bring the face of Christ, the icon of Christ, into the marketplace. Then Christ can come into the place where you work or play or eat. He will come into your home or a restaurant or a school or a company cafeteria or a subway or wherever.

Let me give you an example. When I first came to Canada and America, I had to support my sick husband and our baby, so I had a job as a waitress. That was my duty of the moment. Well, there is a way of being a waitress and there is a way of being a waitress. I'll explain.

It so happened that I was in New York City at a very good restaurant and people from Wall Street would come in every day. One of them was a very fat gentleman who used to eat pies every day. He would eat loads of pies. So, one day, very quietly, I said to him, "You must love God very much, dear sir." He looked at me strangely. Can you imagine anyone saying something like that? He said, "What do you mean?" I said, "Well, you're eating so much of this pie, it will get you back to him fast—before you know it." He looked at me and said, "What you're trying to tell me is that I'm committing suicide through my fork." I said, "Well, I wasn't going to put it that bluntly." I was about three inches away from him, and he looked at me and said, "Lady, you've got something there." And he gave me a five dollar tip. The next day he came in and said, "Okay, what do I eat?" I said, "A salad."

So you see, there is a way to be a waitress and there is a way to be a waitress. He said, "You show very much concern, not only to me, but to that gentleman over there too. He's so thin and you're always feeding him more." I said, "Well, I hope you do not object to my bringing religion into this situation. I believe in God and I believe that God said, 'Love your neighbor as yourself.' So you're fat; I want to make you thin. He is thin; I want to make him fat. That, I think, is loving others." He said, "Gee whiz. I must tell that to my wife." I didn't preach, really. I didn't say I was Catholic or Protestant. I just said, "You're welcome."

My next job was at Macy's, a big department store in New York. I was in the gift shop, where I made more money than I did waitressing. In those days I made twelve dollars a week plus commissions on what I sold. I had the highest commission in all of Macy's. One day the manager of the personnel department said, "Katie, come see me in five minutes." So, I thought to myself, "What's wrong?" I went to his office and he said, "Sit down, Miss de Hueck, and tell me how it is that you make the highest commission." I said to him, "Well, it is very difficult to tell you. First, I'm on the job eight hours a day. I don't go to smoke or take a cup of coffee or tea. I tend to the customers. That's what I was hired for, and, you see, when I accept a contract of this kind, be it just as a humble sales clerk, I make a contract between God, Macy's, and myself." The gentleman said, "What has God got to do with this?" I said, "Oh, God has a lot to do with this business. You see, I would be very ungrateful to my Lord, and to you, if I hid on the job to have a cigarette (I smoked in those days) or a cup of coffee, or talked to the other salesgirls while I let the customers cool their heels. That would be, to me, a sin." The manager said, "Oooooh, we're in the sin business! Well, thank you, miss. I was going to ask you to talk to the staff, to the whole group, but with this sin business and this God business, no, cherie. I'll leave you alone. Just keep on getting the business."

So, you see, this is what I mean. You as a Christian, a follower of Christ, as a mother or father, do your duty of the moment. Whatever your duty is, you do it with great love. And as you do, the image of Christ, the icon of Christ, will be shown to people, wherever you are—in your home, in your place of work outside your home, in your school, in the neighborhood where you live, in your church, in the grocery store, wherever you happen to be.

Now, it's fine to say "Praise the Lord" and so forth. Yes, it's wonderful to praise God. But remember that Christ said, "It's not he who says 'Lord, Lord' who is going to heaven, but those who do the will of my Father" (Mt 7:21). What's the will of the Father? It's so simple. It's the duty of the moment. Now, for your children, the duty of the moment is obedience to you. It's going to school, it's attending to homework. For you, it's supervising your kids when they do homework, and paying attention to them and seeing there are no shenanigans!

There are plenty of good things you can go out and do, programs and such. Perhaps you have made a Marriage Encounter or something. There are all kinds of good Catholic things you can do, but whatever they are, you have to realize that there is always the duty of the moment to be done. And it *must* be done, because the duty of the moment is the duty of God. That's what God calls us to do. And if we do that, do you realize what happens? People follow us. We don't have to preach by word of mouth. We preach by living. We preach by doing. We preach by being.

When I was a waitress, I had a husband and baby to support, so the money was very important to me. One day I saw another waitress swiping twenty-five cents, and she saw me see her swipe it. So she said to me, "I'm sorry." She came to apologize to me. I said to her, "Maybe you need it." She said, "But you have a child. I haven't got one." I said, "Then why did you do it?" She replied, "Oh, I want a new dress." And I said to her, "Well, help yourself." She said, "You're not mad, Katie?" I said, "No. I'm not mad at all. Why should I be mad?" Her values were very poor, but why should I be mad? I wasn't about to preach at her. I didn't have to.

Did you ever consider the patience of Christ? He's patient with us, infinitely patient. Have you ever considered the tenderness of God? He holds each of us, like a baby, in his arms. Have you ever considered his love? People always say, "Yes, he died on the cross." And they go on from there. But remember, before he died, he became a human baby in a woman's belly and he grew for nine months in great darkness. Can your mind absorb the love of God to send his only Son to redeem us in that strange, incredible way? Nine months in the womb of a woman! Then for many years he was obedient to his foster father and his mother. After that, he had several years of public life and preaching, crying in the wilderness, so to speak. Can you hear the wind bringing his words to us? Listen to that wind! You can listen to something else too—Bang! Bang! Bang! That's the sound of a hammer on a nail. That nail is in his flesh! Can you think of that? Then, the crucifixion. Think of all the pain he went through. He died a terrible death—all for us. After that there was his resurrection.

Now, how do you show the face of Christ to a world that is secular, atheistic, indifferent, greedy, and selfish? By doing what he asks you to do. And his voice is very simple. He says, "Love God with your whole life, your whole heart. And love your neighbor as yourself" (Mt 22:38-39). Now, just do as he tells you, and live your life for everybody. The place to start is with the duty of the moment.

Remember also that when you do the duty of the moment, you do something for Christ. You make a home for him, in the place where your family dwells. You feed him when you feed your family. You wash his clothes when you do their laundry. You help him in a hundred ways as a parent. Then, when the time comes when you will appear before Christ to be judged, He will say to you, "I was hungry and you gave me to eat. I was thirsty and you gave me to drink. I was sick and you looked after me" (Mt 25:35-36). Get the picture?

God is a person. He is present in our fellow man, but we don't care. We're not interested in the other fellow. We're only interested in ourselves, so the other sits in utter loneliness, and slowly, slowly, the face of Christ becomes nebulous, vague. We cannot get hold of it. Nobody shows it to us.

There is something each of us has to do, my friends. First I have to be an icon of Christ. Then the icon must step out of my heart and wash the feet of my brother, for Christ said, "I have come to serve you."

Loneliness

Question: A few of us were talking together yesterday about our struggles living as Christians in the kind of world we have and how lonely it is. Can you say something about the loneliness of being a Christian today?

Answer: Yes. In my own life, I have known loneliness. It's like this. You are in love with Christ and you have a passionate desire to make Christ loved by others, to make him understood. You want to share that love with others and there's nobody who seems to understand. Day after day there is this loneliness. It's like a gray, terrible thing that holds you so tight it never seems to let you go. It's almost impossible to explain it, to describe it. I know that from the age of sixteen or so I have been lonely all my life, simply because my first husband was in the war and we were apart. Then, after we came here, he was sick and I had to go away from him and the baby in order to find work to support us. I was earning a living but I was lonely. And then later, Eddie came along and there were only a few years of something different and then he died and loneliness held me tight again.

The only way to be able to function under such loneliness is to understand it. You have to understand that it is the loneliness of Christ that has been given to you. It's as if he gives you a key to his loneliness. For is there anybody who was less lonely than Christ? For God to become a man certainly is lonely. Then, again, walk into Gethsemane and spend time next to him, and you will understand what loneliness is.

I don't consider loneliness a problem; it is part of a gift of God to us. He sends us loneliness to cover our weakness. He sends us loneliness to make us new. He sends us loneliness so that we will turn to our bother and sister and offer our hands to them.

How can I tell you what loneliness is? It is present even between husband and wife, between child and parents; always it stands between them. I think of it as a sort of garden enclosed, to which God alone has access. It's difficult. But everybody is lonely until they meet God.

Comment: When you're dealing with loneliness, it can lead you to God, but I think it also can lead you away from God and into evil. How do you find the good of Christ in loneliness instead of getting crushed by it?

Answer: You have to look at it this way: There is no love without pain. If you love Christ, you will endure pain for him—and loneliness is a kind of pain. Loneliness also can be fruitful for those who follow Christ, because we can share our loneliness with God, if we wish to. The key that opens to you the true essence of loneliness is sharing it with Christ. If you share it with him, how is it possible to be lonely when the two lonelinesses blend together?

When you have faith in the midst of loneliness, you can invite Christ into that loneliness. What I do is invite Christ for coffee. That's my celebrated move. I get my Bible and I open it up and I put a cup of coffee there for him and a cup of coffee here for me. Of course, he isn't there, you see. There isn't anybody there. But I can talk to him that way. So I read the Gospel and I see something in it and I say to him, "Do you really mean that, for us to love as you do? That's impossible!" Then he says, "Yes, it's impossible, but all things are possible with me." That's in another part of the book and I can find that with the little ribbons, see. So I get an answer. You see? You have loads of fun that way. You try it some time. And your kids will have loads of fun. Don't be afraid to try it sometime.

Our Lady, Mary the Mother of Jesus

Question: What do you think of Our Lady? Have you been to her apparition sites?

Answer: Oh yes. I was at Fatima quite a while ago, before it became huge. The bush where she appeared was still there then. Fatima is one of the apparitions approved by the Church as authentic. Of course, you don't have to believe in it [since it doesn't "belong to the deposit of faith" as Christ's own Revelation does (see note below)—Ed.][1], but when you walk with Our Lady with a deep faith in your heart, you really have something. It's impossible to explain. I believe in all of the approved titles the Church gives to Our Lady. But the greatest of these, I believe, is *Theotokos*, Mary the Mother of God. That title makes her very special. She is very helpful in dealing with the devil too. I have a feeling that Our Lady covers all of

---

[1] "Throughout the ages, there have been so-called 'private' revelations, some of which have been recognized by the authority of the Church. They do not belong, however, to the deposit of faith. It is not their role to improve or complete Christ's definitive Revelation, but to help live more fully by it in a certain period of history" (*Catechism of the Catholic Church,* § 67).

Madonna House with her big mantle. Isn't that beautiful? And if this little pipsqueak devil tries to come in, she says, "Uh, uh—you can't come in." And she can cover your home too, if you ask her.

You see, I'm a person of great faith and simplicity. I take Our Lady and the saints into my home. It's very simple. I don't mean that you should. You might not have a devotion to saints, but I pity you if you haven't, because you can have lots of fun being surrounded by them and Our Lady. If you have her around your house, boy, you're the luckiest of mortals. So I always have a picture of her in my place.

Chapter 13

Poverty and Detachment

How does poverty apply to you as married people with families? We have to examine our consciences. We each have to say, what can I give away? What can I give to the poor?

Now, I'm not saying that you have to make a vow or a promise of poverty as some people do. No. But consider this: poverty is a natural development that a person in love with God desires. The meaning of poverty can be summed up in one sentence: to cease to desire any possessions. Poverty means total detachment.

Now, let's put this into very simple language. Here's what it's like. Let's say you're a woman out for a walk—and you pass a shop and you see a gorgeous red dress in the window, and you want the red dress because it's the color for you and it's pretty. And you pray and think a little more about it. Two weeks later, you pass the shop and there is the red dress. You look at it. It's not a bad dress. It's okay, but the desire to possess it is gone, more or less. Two weeks later you pass by again and the red dress is still there, but you don't even notice it. That is how poverty develops itself. It's a desire not to possess anything; not to desire to possess things.

When you examine your conscience about this, also examine your home. Take TV, for example. How many televisions do you need? One in the bedroom, one in the front room, one in the back room, all over the place? Do you really need them all? "But the kids," you say. Well, it's time for parents to control their children.

Next take cars. Look at the ones you've got. Examine each vehicle. Do you need a car for the office and a car for suburbia? Suburbia is getting very expensive to live in these days. Maybe you would be better off not living in suburbia. Perhaps it's better to go into the city and have a smaller house. My friends restored a house in the inner city and it's really beautiful. They laugh at the people in suburbia who have to travel so far, when they live right around the corner from everything.

Well, what you do is up to you. It's a question of detachment, really. It's not a question of "I have" or "I have not." Take one good very wealthy friend who used to come and help us at our Friendship House in Harlem. Her daughter would come too, and her son, to fetch his mother when she was there to visit us.

One day she said to me, "You know, we're very wealthy, Catherine." I said, "Yes, I know." She said, "But I had a very, very wonderful way of doing things when my husband was a diplomat in Great Britain." I said, "You did?" She said, "Yes. You know what I did? I used a black dress. It was a very simple black dress, but I used a lot of costume jewelry, the kind you can buy at the dime store. Everybody thought it was good jewelry because of my family. But it was just junk. And I changed it. I changed a sash here and a hankie there, and I would add a brooch or change a necklace to make it look different, all on the same dress." Here she was, one of the best dressed woman in America, and this is what she did. Then she said, "But everything I saved, I gave to the poor. I had two dresses for the whole season. And my dresses were worth $500. Well, I had two dresses for $1,000, but that was all, and I made them last for a long time. I saved maybe $10,000, which I gave to the poor. Every time I *don't* buy a dress, I always give the money to the poor. Now, I could buy all the dresses I want, but it's the one that I *don't* buy so I can give the money to the poor that I like the best. Now, that's a personal thing that I do." I said, "That's a very good idea." We can all benefit by that.

I have another friend who was a buyer of women's dresses for a big store. She used to go to Paris and she would come back laden with dresses. Because she was a buyer, they were given to her free of charge. One day she went to a Dominican retreat and she called me up later. She said, "Catherine, come down. I want to talk to you, PDQ." So I went and she said, "This is terrible! Look at all these!" She had a big closet with sliding doors and there was one dress after another in it. She said, "Look at them. Look at them! Am I poor? Am I a follower of Jesus Christ? Do you think I'm going to keep all these?" I said, "I hope not." She said, "No, I'm not." And she gave it all away to people—to servants and people who didn't have very much money to buy things. She left herself four dresses.

That's not all she did. After that, she got busy and got the people who paint and wallpaper, and she had them paint her whole place—she had but two rooms—all gray. Gray! I still remember it. She had a beautiful picture of Saint Francis in the middle, and she had red furniture. That is to say she bought second-hand furniture and painted it red. And people used to come and say, "My God, how wonderful." No knickknacks. Peaceful colors. And people started coming to her home, because it was full of peace. She was still earning money, yes, but she was watching things carefully and giving away what she could. She was detached.

Now, it's nice to give it all away if you're single and by yourself, but if you're married, you do it a little differently. You don't have to deprive yourself so you fall into poverty, but just ask yourself "Do I need that?" Ask yourself that question. "Do I really need this? Do I need this TV? Do I need these shoes? Do I?" It's in ways like that, asking questions and giving honest answers, that you can teach yourself about acquisitions, and you'll teach your children too.

Children pick things up very quickly. One day in Arizona a father, mother and their children walked into an ice cream parlor where I was. Yes, there was I, who am talking about deprivation, sitting there having my face filled with ice cream! Well, anyway, the family looked at the ice cream and the father said, "Boys, what are you going to get?" And the older one of the four kids said, "Well, we were talking about the poverty in India. How much are these?" So the clerk said they were fifty cents a cone, three dollars for all of them. So he said, "Daddy, will you give me three dollars so I can give it to the Hindu people, and we'll not get the ice cream?" Well, that was something. The guy who owned the ice cream store heard this and he gave them the ice cream and said, "You don't have to pay for it." So that's what I call preaching the Gospel with your lives. It was preached.

There is another friend I have, a man who also is a millionaire. Sometimes I think he is the poorest man of all. He comes to one of our field houses in the U.S. It's called a listening house, where our staff are there to listen to people who come. And this man comes to our house and he sits at the feet of one of our staff workers, just a young girl of twenty-eight, and he says, "Tell me about Jesus Christ." You see, money does not satisfy him. Something else has entered into his heart. And it should enter into all our hearts.

So we have to examine ourselves. You see, love is the one thing God left us. We really must die to help one another. We have to forget ourselves and serve one another.

Punishment

Question: Catherine, can we have your view on punishment for children?

Answer: A child *wants* to be punished for doing wrong. So it's okay as long as you're not angry and both you and the child know that it's deserved. That's what the psychiatrists say. But one of the worst things is to hit a kid because you're angry.

Permissiveness is not getting us anywhere. Opening the Bible, I see that God the Father in the Old Testament says that it's necessary to chastise a person in order to bring him back to his heart. Somehow or other, man wanders away from God. He, of course, has given us full freedom to go away. Then he says to us, "Well, now that this is done, let us sit around the table and talk things over."

So we have to have some chastisement for the children, but it needs to go with a lot of love, a lot of kindness, and a lot of tenderness—and let me repeat: You must never chastise a child if you are angry. That's something else again.

Let me tell you how I was punished when I was a child. I went and stole apples from the neighbor's yard and my mother told my father about it. He said, "Catherine, you stole some apples from the neighbor's yard." I said, "Yes, I did." He said, "What do you think your punishment should be?" I said, "Well, I should get the switch. I need a switch." He said, "You do? How many times do you want me to switch you?" I thought a lot and said, "I think five times for each apple." Since I had taken two apples, that was ten times. So Father got a little switch and put me on his knees and I counted. One! Two! And so forth. I had tears in my eyes and he said, "Now you have to go apologize to the people next door."

See, I wasn't perfect. Now, my father was not angry. And I was definite that I should be punished because I had done something wrong.

Learning about Confession

Now, this eventually got into the catechetical business. My mother said, "You have to go to confession." She didn't make any big fuss about it. I said, "What's confession?" She said, "Confession is the same thing as telling your father you did something wrong, and that thing is a sin." So I had it explained to me. My mother said, "You go into the church and up to the priest for confession." In Russia we had no confessionals; the priest sat out in the middle of the church. Mother said, "You're a little girl, so he'll probably take you on his lap and he will talk to you. And he will kiss you and it will be like Christ kissing you—the kiss of Christ. So, go."

Well, I was all for that brilliant idea. It sounded good to me, so I went. It was an Orthodox priest. My mother and my father rooted me in both Orthodoxy and Catholicism, and in Russia, of course, we went to the Orthodox Church.

Sure enough, this good, holy priest took me on his lap, and he covered me with his stole. "Now, Catherine," he said, "What have you done?" So I told him about the apples. Mother had said that I should tell him what I did wrong and I thought the apples were really wrong. When I was finished telling him all about the apples, he asked me, "How well do you love your enemies?" The Russians always start with "How well do you love your enemies?"

Well, that was such a new idea to me, I said, "What's an enemy?" He said, "Somebody you don't like." And I said, "Oh, I know a girl at my grade school, Olga, and I don't like her. She always does this and she does that." He said, "Well, God said you must love your enemies." I said, "He did?" The priest said, "That's what he died for, so you'd better start." He explained to me that I should promise to make up with Olga. I wasn't sure I wanted to and I got off his lap and I thought about it very seriously for a few minutes. Then I climbed back on his lap and I said, "Okay, I will." So he gave me absolution, blessed me, and kissed me on the forehead. And that was my first confession.

I went home, looked at Mother with my nose up like this, you know. I said, "I've been kissed by Christ. Christ kissed me. It's really something!" Today, sixty years later, at my age, I still think of confession as the kiss of Christ. I can't forget it.

Father was just saying a little while ago that before Vatican II everybody was afraid to go to confession. Now they're not afraid any more, but they don't want to go at all. Of course nobody should be afraid of God. God is merciful. God is mercy itself. Nobody should be afraid of confession. I run to

confession, zippity do da. Why? Because here's what happens:
Christ in the priest forgives me. He is mercy. And in that
sacrament, there is God's mercy itself. In Russia, the priest
doesn't say "I absolve you." He says "Christ absolves you." So
it's very clear and there's no problem, at least there is none for
me. I've always thought that confession is the kiss of Christ. So
at Madonna House, when confessions are heard, I say to
everyone, "Go and get kissed by Christ," and the kids all look
at me, with their big eyes, and so I tell them this story and
explain it to them.

You see, the thing is this: We are in an entirely different
civilization and any given father and mother really have a lot to
overcome. It's substantial. When you belong to Christ, you're
going to be different. Not everybody belongs to him, but you do.
So, you be different—stand up and be counted. You are parents.
You are up against hell let loose, that's all. You have the life of
a child, or perhaps many children, in your hands. It is a big
responsibility.

The Responsibility to Discipline

I remember when I was a child one day my mother put me
in a corner to punish me. I had done something wrong, so I was
being punished for it. I turned around from the corner and I said,
"Mummy, what right have you got to put me in that corner?" I
really wanted to know. There was no offense meant, you
understand. And Mother looked at me. She was very confused.
She couldn't believe she had a child like me, I suppose.

She said, "I entered into wedlock; I married your father.
The day I married him, I prayed that he and I would have
children, and you're one of them. But I knew while I prayed that
the reason I should have children was so that I could lead them
to Christ. So naturally, when you're disobedient, I have to
chastise you so that you, in the act of going in the corner, are
obedient to Christ. For when you are obedient to me, you are
obedient to Christ."

Well, that really made me think and I forgot the time. In
fact, I thought about that so much that I stayed in the corner a

whole hour. I was supposed to stay a half hour in that place and I stayed a whole hour. It was something to think about, eh? So, my mother was right.

Teen Discipline

Question: Today there is a complex society. When I grew up, we had other adults in the community who, if you stepped out of line outside of your own home, would give you the back of their hand to keep you in line. They did this because the same discipline applied in the whole neighborhood as inside your own house. There was continuity in what was expected from children. Today that is gone. Children today can tell you what their rights are very well, especially teenagers. In school and outside of the home, they get hit with different ideas and they are told these are their rights, that they should be free to express themselves. How can we combat that?

Answer: First, by example. Second, by Jesus Christ. Let's say a teenager, a young person of nineteen or twenty comes to me at Madonna House and says, "I'm so darn tired of planting carrots that I just won't do it." I say, "That's fine. That's very good. Just take the bus home. Goodbye." But that's not what he wants to do. He wants to stay, but he's trying to test me. That's one way.

Another way, he says the same thing, "I don't want to do carrots." And I say, "Well, that's okay. Have you discussed it with God?" He says, "What do you mean, with God?" I say, "It's a very simple thing. You see, you're going to plant carrots, right? Next year a bunch of kids like you will eat them, because you plant carrots in order to feed people." I say, "Do you think God approves of the idea that you don't want to do it?" The average teenager can't stand that, face to face with me, and with another bunch of teenagers who *are* planting carrots.

So then, we have a little seminar at night on the topic "What is Obedience?" Well, it's quite a little seminar. They say, "Look, B, this is impossible," about whatever it is they're supposed to do. "We don't even have a TV here." Well, we do have a TV in the basement, but they don't have time to look at it. I say, "No, we don't have much time for the TV in the basement. You look at it at night or on Sunday. But, what's a TV?" I tell them, "Do you know something, you guys give me the creeps. You don't want to sacrifice anything." And I get a huge, big crucifix and stick it next to the TV. I say, "Have a look at that, and turn off your TV." Sheepishly, they do.

I use dramatic situations like this all the time, you see. Maybe it won't work for you; maybe you can't; but I think you can. You see, one of the things is to challenge them. American and Canadian kids are quite challengeable. I say, "So what—are you going to be a sissy? Are you just going to conform? Are you going to wear your hair long because everybody wears their hair long? And what do you expect out of it? Why did you come to Madonna House? You're not getting any place. You're just not jogging toward Christ." We have a conversation like that.

There is something you always have to remember. You are going to be hit like this. You and your wife or your husband. You're going to be hit. That's natural. Christ was hit. I was hit. You will be hit too, but to follow Christ means you're going to be radical. So let's stand back and deliver. Deliver! Deliver the message, the Good News! Tell your neighbors and friends and family and your children where you stand, and let people know you stand where you do because you believe in Jesus Christ.

What Is Discipline, Anyway?

Discipline comes from the Latin word *disciplinabilis,* "capable of being disciplined or instructed, teachable." From this word also comes the word *disciple,* "pupil, one who receives instruction from another, a learner—especially one who accepts the doctrines of his or her teacher and assists in spreading them."

Here we have the whole idea in a nutshell, for aren't we all disciples of Christ, and mustn't we all so live and have our being as to adhere to and accept his teachings fully, and disseminate them both by example and word? For his teachings are a religion, a way of life, to be believed and lived to the hilt.

How can this be possible without a slow, constant, growing strength of character? It begins with the adult. We must first be capable of "being disciplined or instructed" ourselves. Are we? Do we give our children the example of a life anchored in the great tranquillity of God's order? Of complete, instantaneous obedience to his laws and those of the Church? Does our will function as one directed by a reason illuminated by our holy faith? Is it a firm, unshakable will, that will sooner allow the body that houses it to die than deviate one iota from the teachings of our Lord and God?

Or do we preach one thing to our children and do another? Do our lofty words jibe with our everyday life and deeds? How can we expect obedience, charity, selflessness from our children if we do not possess them ourselves?

Thus it falls on the parents not only to transmit and assist in spreading Christ's teachings by their words in their homes, but to integrate those teachings into their daily lives, and to demand the same from their children.

For without the holy virtue of obedience, without the shining virtue of charity, without selflessness, there is no possibility that we or our children will become true disciples of the Lord. Unless children learn from their very birth obedience, charity, selflessness, the world will perish and we with it!

Let us therefore bring back to its fulness, its beauty, and its glory the word *discipline*. Let us make her the constant companion of our home life, becoming through her, teachable, instructable, disciples of Christ, whose life is spent adhering closely to his holy laws and doctrines and passing them on, disseminating them first to our own, then to the world at large.

So What's Education?

Education is synonymous with so many things. It means, of course, the gathering of knowledge, primarily the knowledge of God and his laws and truths, on which all other knowledge must be built. It also means shaping and molding a young soul in the likeness of its Savior, who is our ultimate and perfect model. It means tempering a young, pliant will, grafting it onto an intellect and reason illuminated by faith. And it means forming a character, making the child of today a worthy citizen of tomorrow. Frankly, education starts at birth and ends at death.

Today I want to go more deeply into home education—not just "teaching children their prayers at the knee of their mother," but something deeper.

Let us first take the brotherhood of man under the fatherhood of God. It teaches that through the Incarnation and Redemption of Christ all men and women have become brothers and sisters of one another and of Christ, and thus children of his and our Father in heaven. This is a theological truth. Do you believe it? Do you teach it to your children? For home is the place they will learn it. Are you educating your children in your home in this great verity of our faith, teaching them to make it part and parcel of their life, upholding them even when its results are painful to them, as sometimes they may be? For it takes courage, faith, and fortitude, not to mention justice and charity, to go against the current and treat our fellow human beings, all of them, as brothers and sisters.

Then there is the next step, the luminous doctrine of the Mystical Body of Christ, which teaches that every human being baptized in the name of the Father and of the Son and of the Holy Spirit into the holy Catholic Church is a member of the Mystical Body of Christ, of which Christ is the head. This intensifies, enlarges, and lifts up to eternity the first truth of our being brothers and sisters, making all Christians irrespective of color, nationality, language, ethnic origin, situation, age, or mental or physical capacity part of us. Oh, what love, what patience and perseverance, what example must go into educating one's children in this all-encompassing truth of our holy faith, the foundation of that restoration of the world to Christ that you and I dream of ...

For if ever we of the faith lived this doctrine, the non-believers, the potential members of the Mystical Body of Christ, would desire with a great desire to enter its glorious unity and become one with the fold.

Just think, this conversion, this desire, depends on you and on the education you give to your children. What an enormous responsibility! And it is all yours.

Then the third truth: Do you teach your children to see Christ in their neighbor? Their poor, sick, rich, black, white, yellow, born, unborn neighbor? Remember, "Whatsoever you do to the least of my brothers you do to me" (Mt 25:40). That encompasses the world and every human being in it.

What a vision to open before the innocent, beautiful eyes of one's children! What a heritage of love to give them! Are you doing it? For on these three points, these three cardinal truths of our faith, rests the political, economic, and spiritual reformation, regeneration, and restoration of our sick and sad world. Are you doing your part in this? Is your home the school of love that it should be?

Taking Time for Attention

Another thing the kids want when they come here to us is attention. They want personal attention from papa and mama, but that doesn't happen at home, so they come here. A young man expects papa to sit down, open an editorial, so he and papa can discuss the editorial. When they are here, they come to me with an editorial. They say, "B…" (they call me B), "have you read this editorial?" I always have time. (Actually, I never have time, but I always find it.) So I'm reading the editorial that I read yesterday and they're so full of it. Then after we talk, they say, "Ah, now I got Katie to read that editorial. She agrees with me. All is well." Do you know what I mean? I've given them some attention. It seems that they desire it.

Now, there is another situation I want to put before you as plainly as it is. How many of your daughters have had an abortion? This is something that every mother should know. But mothers don't know this. We had a girl here who had two abortions in a year and a half. I sat with her for about three hours. I said, "Did you tell your mother?" Oh, no, she hadn't. "Sweetheart," I said, "You have to tell your mother. Your mother brought you into this world, and your father." It took three and a half hours to convince her, and I still don't know if she has told her mother. It seems as if those things pass by and parents don't even know anything about them. That they should tell us—me or anybody at Madonna House—amazes us. Why should we know? So I asked this girl, "Why do you tell me?" Well, she said, "I had to tell somebody," to which I replied, "That somebody is your mother." And she said "Oh, no, no, no." And I ask you why?

Now, I just had to lay that down before you because it's so common at Madonna House lately. It's not as if you stand accused. Not at all. I simply beg you to pay more attention to your children, to pray for them, to bring them that glass of water. "Mommy, can I have a glass of water?" That's where to start. Pay attention to them.

I feel so deeply for all of you, especially parents with little children. Watch over your children. Watch them. Hold them tight. Never mind about getting lots of money. Get a smaller house. Don't have the wife work; let her stay home. This has nothing to do with women's lib; this is for the salvation of the family.

Part 3

Family Feasts and Seasons

Chapter 14

Advent

Let's begin at the beginning of the Church year, which is the beautiful season of Advent. Advent, of course, is the season of waiting, waiting for the Savior to appear. It brings to mind Mary's time of waiting, the time of her expectancy, her pregnancy.

Many of us married folks know what it's like to wait for a new baby to come. Pregnancy, an advent eternally renewed in every woman expecting a child, is a book written by the hand of God, with each page, each day, each hour, reminding us of the first Advent. Think of the very first moment of the first Advent, when worlds were hushed and angels still—waiting, waiting for the answer of a young girl, the young Mary! Her "yes" to God, spoken so softly as to be almost a whisper, shook heaven and earth, and began the ineffable, incomprehensible, most beautiful mystery of the Incarnation! "Let what you have said be done to me." (See Lk 1:38.)

Each pregnancy sings of the first Advent. Each is a time of waiting, of joy so immense that it can only be encompassed by the eyes and soul of a woman in love and filled with the fruit of that love.

How softly our advents come to us women. They herald their coming with a kiss. They speak louder, through the tender embrace of a man's arms. They sing their Te Deums, "We praise you, O God, ... " in a voice of thunder at the ecstasy of love, for it takes *three* to bring to us mortals our advents—a man, a woman, and God! At the last echoes of our Te Deum, the peace that surpasses all understanding comes to dwell with us, for where love is, God is, and there his peace dwells. Peace, stillness, and Mary's lullaby bring us sleep that gives us strength for the thousand tasks of tomorrow, and prepares us for the infinite graces to come.

Then there is pregnancy, the time of waiting. And for us women, the time of pain too. The discomforts of the first months, the fears that steal into our minds in the night, these foreshadow the real pain to come, for it is written that "in pain we shall bear our children" (Gn 3:16). It is also the time of expectant love. Like the child in our wombs, in the dark of its prenatal night, our love grows. Perfect love casts out all fears and changes pain into joy. That is the tremendous secret that Christ, the fruit of the first Advent, has given the world. That is the secret of the folly of the Cross that comes to those of us who accept our advents with the same holy joy God has in sending them to us!

Slowly, the litany of the days of our pregnancy unfolds itself. Its accents grow each day, the notes of an unfinished symphony that will find the majesty of its completion only with the first cry of our new-born child. It begins with an exultant chord. We mortal women are sure we shall bear the fruit of our love. Then the symphony softens and almost dies—into a plaintive melody of half-guessed shadows, of half-felt pains. Next it lifts itself up into the theme that grows and grows, only to pause in the utter stillness of one dying chord of wonder at the first sign of life within our womb, and to become a new, slow, majestic magnificat like Mary's, "My soul magnifies the Lord ... " (Lk 1:46-55), a hymn of growing love and gratitude to God. It chants the final movement in notes of joy, all wet with tears; and ends again in the strange exultation of an infant's cry that re-echoes God's voice, pure and clear on this earth.

Advent and pregnancy are the time of waiting, the time of the great prayer of silence we women know, of utter humility and holy tranquility, of a strange union with God the Father, from whom all paternity comes, a time of living with Mary and learning from her all there is to learn about expectant motherhood and motherhood fulfilled!

Such is pregnancy, for us women. One thing is especially incomprehensible—why so many among us refuse it.

Chapter 15

Christmas

Now at this time Caesar Augustus issued a decree for
a census of the whole world to be taken.... So Joseph
set out from the town of Nazareth in Galilee and
travelled up to Judaea ... in order to be registered
together with Mary, his betrothed, who was with
child. While they were there, the time came for her to
have her child, and she gave birth to a son, her first-
born. She wrapped him in swaddling clothes, and laid
him in a manger because there was no room for them
in the inn (Lk 2:1, 4-8).

The birthday of Christ! Here is the first page of a love story
never surpassed, about God and the soul of man, God's Bride.
Christmas is the first love letter of God to man, a love letter
called the Incarnation.

Christmas! Here are the first notes, soft and tender and
joyous, of the Song of Songs sung by Christ to his beloved. It is
a song that will end in the whisper of God dying on the Cross,
a death whisper and still a love whisper, the last page of his love
story—his love letter—the last proof of his incomprehensible,
divine love for us!

Christmas is the feast of children and all those who are
childlike and hence able to see God in an Infant in a manger! It
is the feast of home and family reunion. It seems somehow

symbolic of our ultimate reunion with God in our final and true home, our lasting city on the eternal hills of the Lord.

Christmas is the white, immaculate feast of winter, the feast that foretells the white immaculateness of the Host, the helpless Lover who waits unto the end of time to become, himself, the cradle of newly-born souls of his grace.

Christmas is Mary's feast, too, and St. Joseph's, mother and foster father to Fair Love. Consider the Holy Family. They were a poor family, a seemingly ordinary family, a simple, hidden family.

Christmas is the novitiate through which all wedded lovers must pass to make the most of their holy and awesome vocation to love! For to love God, each other, their children, and their neighbors in God, they too must possess the spirit of poverty, chastity, and obedience that Christ preached in his Gospels, the three outstanding virtues of the home of Nazareth,.

It is high time that we Catholics of the twentieth century and beyond got rid of the false notion that poverty, chastity and obedience belong exclusively to those called publicly by God and his Church to the state of perfection. No. These keys to heaven, these *counsels of perfection* (which just means counsels of love), belong in their utter simplicity to *all* baptized Christians, to each according to his or her state of life, for to each Christ said, "Be ye perfect as my Father is perfect" (Mt 5:48).

They belong especially to the Catholic family. Why especially to the family? Because the family should be a school of love for the parents, who through their vocation of love for one another and for God, teach love (which is sanctity) to their children.

Parents must become saints themselves, as well as a school of sanctity and love for their children. Without the practice of the counsels of perfection according to their wedded state, this cannot be achieved. If this is not achieved, then the call to one of the most sublime vocations of God, the vocation to matrimony—a sacrament—will not be fecund in the Lord. To be unfecund is to be sterile, unfulfilled, the greatest tragedy that can befall human beings! Moreover, unless the family is a school of love, of sanctity, whence will we get vocations to the priesthood or religious life, of which it is the cradle?

Where better could the family learn the deep, wonderful lessons of the counsels of perfection than at the manger of the poor Christ, with the chaste and obedient Mary and Joseph? Let us now consider each of the evangelical counsels as they pertain to married couples.

Poverty of Spirit

What does poverty of spirit really mean, in terms of a modern Catholic family? It means, first of all, utter detachment from all created goods. It means a deep, lasting realization that all created things, which includes father, mother, children, relatives and friends, as well as money, house and goods are given to us by God as means to one end, which is *sanctity*. That means our personal and collective sanctity, both as a family and as individuals. Without sanctity we shall not achieve the primary end for which we were created—the Beatific Vision, to see God "face to face" (1 Cor 13:12).

Oh, if only we married folks could learn fully this poverty of spirit! How changed our lives would be! How quickly would each one of us and our family be fully "restored to Christ," and since we are each a unit of society, how quickly would the whole world crane and turn its face to the God who created it! Peace would be ours and happiness that we never dreamed of, for it would bring the kingdom of God to where it belongs since its beginnings, right here on our parched and tired earth.

To use all created goods and creatures as they were meant to be used, to have our heart set in God in total surrender to his most holy will, that is to be poor in spirit. To love all things and all people in him and to be always ready to surrender either, if he so wishes—that is to be poor in spirit. To remember that all we need is money enough for our needs, and that anything we have beyond that belongs in justice to our neighbor in need, the poor of Christ; and to stop trying to keep up with the Joneses, who, spiritually speaking, typify the world, the flesh and the devil—that is to be poor in spirit. To be detached from all, deep inside ourselves, and attached to God and his most holy will, trustful in his word, abandoned to the designs of his Divine Providence, in utter simplicity of faith—that is to be poor in spirit. That is to be free, to be whole, to be happy and at peace with the world. Christmas is truly the school of that spirit.

Chastity

The second counsel, chastity, is usually applied to single people only. Yet, what our sensual world needs today is chastity, as it is applied to both single and married people. There is a special chastity for married folks. It consists in fidelity to their marriage vows, in faithfulness to one another, in modesty that remembers that each belongs to the other until death, and that neither can in speech, act, dress, or any other way, have any dealings with members of the opposite sex that, even in their shadowy connotations, savor of an imperfection against this shining, glorious virtue.

It would take a book to define in detail the fragile, fragrant and exquisite virtue of marital chastity to our lustful, forgetful world that worships the body beautiful as a god unto itself, a world in which men and women spend millions on face and body—and not to attract their own husbands and wives either, but other people's. What better book can there be, though, than Bethlehem? With the most chaste and pure man who was also God, lying, a Child in the crib, surrounded by the *Immaculata*, his virgin mother, and Joseph, his virginal foster father. These holy three will gladly and easily explain all about the spirit of chastity to anyone who comes to them to find out.

Obedience

Obedience is a forgotten virtue in our day, yet the most needed, for its opposite reigns supreme in our age. Disobedience is the sin of Satan, whose one aim is to make split personalities of all of us so that he better can get hold of us and rule over us.

How does he achieve this aim? Very simply—by offering us the same old polished apple he gave our first parents, Adam and Eve—the apple of disobedience.

Behold our modern world. Parents obey neither the laws of God nor of man. Or they try to get out from under them while rendering lip service to both. Naturally, in their homes, children will not obey. Behold the fruits of all this chaos: juvenile delinquency, gangs, youths in prison for murder, divorce courts jammed, and nations crumbling before their foes like houses of cards the world over because, being composed of units of single families undermined by the termites of disobedience, they have lost the will to fight.

Poverty of spirit, chastity in and out of wedlock, and obedience for all, but especially for families—that is the curriculum of the novitiate of Bethlehem. That is the school of love, of which Christmas is the first beautiful page, the first soft, joyous note of its song.

Put Christ back into Christmas, and bring families back to Christ, the Christ of Bethlehem; this is the way of survival for all of us, but especially for the family. Let us arise now and go with the Magi to Bethlehem before it is too late, so that, falling down and adoring our Lord and God, we may begin to learn the lessons of love, without which we shall perish.

Chapter 16

Epiphany

Epiphany means "manifestation"—the manifestation of God to his people, his manifestation of himself to the Magi.

> After Jesus had been born in Bethlehem in Judaea, ... some wise men came to Jerusalem from the east. "Where is the infant king of the Jews?" they asked. "We saw his star as it rose and have come to do him homage." ... There in front of them was the star they had seen rising; it went forward and halted over the place where the child was. The sight of the star filled them with delight, and going into the house they saw the child with his mother Mary, and falling to their knees they did him homage. Then, opening their treasures, they offered him gifts of gold and frankincense and myrrh (Mt 2:1-2, 9-11).

Epiphany: the journey across verdant valleys, mountains, wide and narrow roads, dangerous waters and quiet streams, deserts and fruitful fields, undertaken by the Magi because of an immense and strange star which they followed, and which led them to a stable with a man, a woman and a Child!

How long a journey for the Magi? No one can tell; the Magi are dead. The Magi were wise, with the wisdom of man and grace. They followed the song of their wisdom and came within the center of light—blinding light. And light brought faith, and faith brought love, and love gave gifts of myrrh and frankincense and gold.

Two emptied loves met: God's, who emptied himself in a Child, and men's, who emptied themselves of all that was not love, not God.

God, who is Love, showed the Magi himself, a Child. They took love away and returned whence they came. And as they went, they became lights, because they burned with love. They truly were the Lord's first apostles, these three Gentiles to whom he manifested himself on that day. They came and they went, and left no trace for men to see. But oh! The beauty of their footsteps in the sands of time, visible to God alone. He loved it so that he gave it to his Bride, the Church, to cherish and to love, to have and to hold unto the end of time. She called it Epiphany, and held its wisdom, faith, and love for all her countless children, that they might learn how to travel far, led by the immense and strange star of faith, the faith that leads to the feet of him who is her Love, our God.

Epiphany is the feast that in so many countries is called "the family feast." How did it come to be that?

Behold now a man. Behold a maid, both as yet asleep in their youth and virginity. And then see them awaken and find a strange and immense star in each other's eyes. Keep on looking, and you will see them pursue their journey through stormy seas and quiet waters, narrow and wide roads, deserts and verdant fields and valleys. How long a journey for the man and the maid? Again, no one can tell. They keep it all to themselves. They come to the starlit shelter that is an altar. There, dressed in beauty, they pledge their love.

The man, the maid, they pledge their love, and there you see they bend and lay their first gift at their Lord's tiny feet. It is frankincense, containing all their ecstasy and joy.

Time goes by, and they are still in Bethlehem, kneeling before his crib. And now he smiles and gives them back a gift, for he is never outdone in generosity. He gives himself, in their first-born child. And now, like the Holy Family, they also are three—a man, a woman, and a child.

Time runs on, as men know time, and the gift of myrrh is laid at his holy feet. For their years are filled with it, the bittersweet herb of pains shared, doubts vanquished, and temptations overcome. They bend once more and empty themselves before his utter helplessness in the love they share and know.

Smilingly, he fills their hearts. Behold their wealth of children and of love! And yet, they still remain, kneeling in the dim stable, on the straw. For they must lay the gold he gave them, all of it, at his feet. They do. Now they arise and go to show to others what they have seen and touched. Behold them now, they who were two but are now many in one, apostles of love beheld, fulfilled, and fruitful. The husband and the wife now take Epiphany from the Church, his Bride, and make it their own, that they may give a star to others on the way. Yes, Epiphany is the feast of the family.

Chapter 17

The Presentation—Candlemas and the Family

And when the day came for them to be purified, as laid down by the Law of Moses, they took Jesus up to Jerusalem to present him to the Lord, observing what stands written in the Law of the Lord: "Every first-born male must be consecrated to the Lord" (Lk 2:22-23).

Behold! The Mother of God, full of grace, vessel of purity! Behold her with St. Joseph and the infant Christ at the Temple! What a lifetime of meditation is encompassed in that one event, that one act of hers, especially when it is linked with the other name of the feast, Candlemas. That is short for "Candle Mass," the Mass at which candles are blessed by priests for us, the laity, to highlight our human existence on this earth. The candles symbolize Mary's purity because traditionally they are made of pure beeswax made by virginal bees.

Indeed, a lifetime of meditation is encompassed in the feast of the Presentation, in Candlemas, for all of us Catholics, but especially for the husband and wife, the married folks!

Consider this: We bring the blessed candles home with us on this joyous feast to light the highlights of our life with their blessed light. We should bring them out for liturgical feasts to make our understanding and our joy in them ever deeper. Is anyone sick among us? The soft light of these blessed candles will bring hope when we light them during administration of the sacrament of the Anointing of the Sick. It will light the path of the dying as they receive the Lord their God in holy Communion.

And in between times each pure, white candle lies near at hand waiting to be lit, like each of us, for aren't we all "blessed candles of the Lord" when we come out of the baptismal font, children of his blinding Light?

Or, to put it another way, consider a youth and a girl as if they are two of God's candles, as yet unaware of their final vocation, as if they are two blessed candles waiting to be lit! It happens so simply. Maybe at a little party their friends throw. Maybe at a big dance. Maybe out skating or at some summer resort. Who can tell? But wherever it is, suddenly each is lit with the flame of love for the other! A vocation is born, the vocation to love in the married state. It is, perhaps, a little flame, wavering in the winds of many emotions, a few fears, a gust or two of uncertainty. Then one day the flame shoots higher and becomes steadier! The youth and the girl both suddenly know it is true. They say so to each other, thus clothing their love with the flesh of the spoken word.

Then comes the day when their love becomes visible and substantial to all, as they stand before the altar of the Lord of light, the Lord who has lit them, his blessed candles, with the flame of love! In voices clear and steady, they pledge their troth before his face for life, until death do them part!

Bright is their flame, steady and sure, as only real, true love can be, burning with the radiance of perfect purity of intention. They realize better than ever, and yet not fully, that if they are to be true to this vocation they are entering into at this holy, hushed moment, they themselves have to be as candles before him. And they have to lead each other to him from whom they have come, constantly, unflinchingly, no matter how hard the winds of life blow about them. They have to burn themselves out in his service, in this vocation and no other.

Then comes the supreme human experience of divine light! Then comes certainty in faith and deed. It happens when two lights shed from two candles melt into one flame the light of which reaches into heaven and, for an instant blends with the light of him who is All Light, because he is All Love, because he is God!

From this merging of light, of man, woman, and God, comes a new light, a child. (It takes three to bring forth into our dark earth a new candle of the Lord, a child!)

Life goes on. There comes the time of watchfulness, for these candles—this man and woman united in the beautiful vocation of matrimony—must guard constantly, zealously, and jealously the purity, the evenness, the constancy of their lights. Slowly into their lives come strange gusts of the cold winds of temptation. Drafts out of depths they did not even suspect existed try to blow out their light with clammy breaths! This is the time to shield the light with the glass of faith. This is the time to set it out of the reach of drafts, on the shelf of utter trust and confidence in God.

Still, life goes on. The tall candles are surrounded by two, three, then four, five, and maybe six little ones! Who can tell how many will be begotten by their upsurge of love, of flame, of union that merges with God's fire and light?

Strange! Suddenly they notice that they, the candles, have decreased, while their flames have increased in size, light, and warmth. They seem to grow smaller, and their light brighter and more beautiful every day because the light of the little candles increases around them.

Then the day comes when there is a sudden burst of flame—all pure flame with no wax left—and their light seems to die! All that is left to see is a coffin standing in the aisle of a church surrounded by six tall candles! But into the bosom of All Light, a light speeds joyously to flame in glory for eternity! Yes, a soul to be presented to the Almighty, a soul perfect and pure, on this feast of the Presentation, the feast of the Purification, Candlemas.

They go together, these celebrations. And for those who have eyes to see and ears to hear, they will offer sources of meditation for a lifetime, especially, it seems, for married folks.

Chapter 18

St. Joseph, Patron of Families
March 19

St. Joseph is patron of the universal Church, patron of a happy death, and a special friend of saintly nuns. To him most of the faithful have a simple, direct devotion, but to them he remains, for the most part, a shadowy, patriarchal figure who forms a silent, protective background to Jesus and Mary. He is much loved, yet little known. St. Joseph is, somehow, taken for granted, but he should not be.

Who defined his age? Why is he usually depicted as an elderly, greying man? It could not be so. Carpentry is not the occupation of oldsters. It demands alert, creative brains, tough, good muscles, craftsmanship, and, in many cases, imagination and artistry. Old men who have made their living at it can, in their old age, putter with it, but not make a livelihood for their families out of it. And St. Joseph did—in a small, poor village at that. And who is there more careful of their pennies than the poor folks? Who demands as much for as little as they do? They must, because when they spend a few dollars for a table or some chairs, they want them well-made and strong, to last a long, long time, in daily use, by many children. Have you ever seen little village folk buy anything? They touch the fabrics. They examine the workmanship. They weigh and measure carefully, for they had to work hard for what they have. They are not going to squander their hard-earned money on flimsy stuff or shoddy workmanship. Not they.

It is such that Joseph served. What he did was well done. He knew all about marginal poverty. Not destitution. No. But poverty. Also he was an artist, a craftsman at his trade. For, what else could God's foster father have been? And so he could not have been old, but in his prime. He was master in his own house, gravely courteous and spare of speech with customers, yet polite and kind. He must have sat at night at his well-made gates, after the manner of the East, discussing slowly the affairs of the village with other men. He was respected by them. Men like him always are.

But there was another side to St. Joseph—the hidden side. For he must have been the first contemplative, living as he did with God hidden under the veil of flesh. There must have been moments when the glory of God was revealed to him. Perhaps it was when he held the Child Jesus in his arms, or looked into his eyes and was filled with the great love of God that enveloped him constantly, but of which he was, perhaps, not always cognizant—for how could a human being, even St. Joseph, live on earth and sustain always the blinding light of God's love?

Joseph, the teacher of silence. He must have used words only when strictly needed, so that his words were of pure gold, words refined in the furnace of the silent love that dwelt with him constantly in his foster Son.

Joseph, the man of utter faith, complete trust, and total surrender to the will of God. Joseph, who heard the voice of angels in his dreams, yet lived the perfectly hidden life of humility that loses itself in simplicity.

March 19 is, therefore, a patronal feast of the family. For to St. Joseph, both husband and wife should go to learn silence, which is so needed in family life today. Joseph will teach them a silence that is warm and loving—a silence that is filled with a charity beyond words. Silence kills little irritations before they become gaping wounds that may break up the bonds of love. A silence that understands. Upholds. Heals. Thousands are the occasions when husbands and wives must go to St. Joseph to learn that kind of holy silence.

And go to him when you have jealousy. Yes, jealousy, that spawn of hell that slithers into the bosom of family life. It slithers in unheard, unnoticed, even as the serpent entered Paradise. Jealousy is the death of trust, the trust that is the first fruit of true love and utter surrender to one another and God. St. Joseph must be invoked. For who more than he had reason for jealousy? Didn't he find his betrothed with child, when they had never come together? He knew it could not have been his child. Yet no sign of jealousy is reported by the austere story of the Gospel. Being a just man, a kind man, a forgiving man, Joseph thought of putting her away quietly. But when the angel spoke in his dream, he trusted. He believed. Without any shadows, without any doubts, against all the evidence of his eyes. And he was asked to believe so much, trust so much. And he did.

What a lesson to wedded lovers! Let them go to St. Joseph when the slithering, snake-like hissing sound of jealousy and mistrust of one another is beginning to be heard in their hearts. He will share with them his faith and trust, and it will restore their love to them whole and stronger than it was before.

When death enters the warm circle of the family, let them turn to St. Joseph, patron of happy death and of life. For he died in the arms of God, who is Life Everlasting, and he can bring the feel of those divine arms to those who have lost the warmth of loving human ones!

The family, even as the individual, must "know God through love, in order to reach him." But love has for a footstool humility and simplicity. Let the family go to Joseph, the carpenter of Nazareth, and ask him to make them into such footstools, for well does that holy carpenter know these two. Skilfully his strong hands will do the work, and easily will he bring the family these two virtues, because he knows that if they possess them, they will possess God, his foster Son.

Let, then, March 19 become a patronal feast of families. Little churches of Christ that families are, they should adopt the patron of the big, universal Church, Bride of Christ, for their own.

Chapter 19

Lent

Slowly, like a song as yet muted by distance, Lent casts its purple shadow on the joyous festivities of Epiphany and Candlemas, the Feast of the Presentation, that are yet filled to the brim with the echoes of Christmas alleluias!

This is as it should be, for Christmas is the beginning of Christ's passion. What else could the Incarnation mean but that God took upon himself the prison of human flesh and began his incomprehensible, ineffable Song of Songs, his song of love that would never end on this earth, until the end of all time. What do we know of this song of love which God, through the liturgical seasons of the year, brings back to us so beautifully? How many of us listen to it with all our minds, all our hearts, and all our souls? How many steep themselves in its sublime melody? How many, listening, are lifted in an ecstasy of joy; and, arising at long last from their sleep, make their lives an answering song that blends and melts in God's? We should answer, for only by singing back our love song to him can we become one harmonious whole—whole men, whole women—and make this crazy, sick world whole again.

Lent can teach us, better than any liturgical season, how to begin to sing back our love song to Christ with the notes of our lives, each clear, each true to the pitch of his ineffable symphony! For Lent is the heart, the essence of his love song. To all those whose ears are open to hear it, he gives its notes with a passion of love that cannot but arouse their love in return.

99

Lent is the heart of love. It is obedience unto death. It is God so in love with a soul that, for the sake of his beloved, he enters his passion to end on a bleak, rough cross, from which the last heart-rending melody is sung in drops of his precious Blood falling slowly as the final notes, and the infinite proof of the heights and depths of Love Incarnate.

Lent is the best novitiate of love. It will graduate us into the sublime school of love—the Mass—which was born of the same love, within its holy season at the Last Supper.

Lent is all of this, for all of us. But for husband and wife especially it is so; because they, in our tragic century, above all other lay people, must steep themselves, fill themselves, with its spirit of sacrifice, obedience, and love. For these three—sacrifice, obedience, and love—are the very essence, the very foundation of their whole vocation. It is for this end that the Lord of Hosts called them to the most holy state of matrimony. It is for this that they received the awesome sacrament of Matrimony. They are God's natural and supernatural teachers in the marketplace of these forgotten virtues that are the soul of Christianity.

Behold our world today! If we look at it with eyes touched by the grace of truth, we shall at once see that Lucifer, crafty general that he is, has pinpointed his attacks on the children of God's blinding light of love and truth on the family.

Insidious and constant is his attack on sacrifice. Gadget after gadget makes life easy for mother. The gadgets give her more time—time to do what? Is it just more time to spend within the shadow of his darkness, in an endless round of so-called "social" activities, that lead her slowly but surely away from home, away from the very heart of her vocation?

Comfort and ease undreamed of by our ancestors, and in itself neither good nor bad, he urges us to use for the softening of our will. Mortifications and penances are fast becoming merely words. The average Catholic has to look them up in a special dictionary to understand them. Plain sacrifice for the sake of one another within the family circle is becoming rarer and rarer. Each family member these days is lulled into being more and more

intent on doing what he wants, when he wants, as he wants
—father, mother and children included. The delicate shadings of
love expressed in forgetting the pronoun *I* in thinking of parents
first and brothers and sisters next, can well nigh disappear.

The "sacrifice" involved in good manners is in danger of
becoming a memory held in the minds of grandparents. Modern
progressive education, with a disregard of will-training and
discipline, can help bring chaos into the home and deal a death
blow to sacrifice. Selfishness becomes the shadow of each
member of the family when it comes to dwell with them.

Love of pleasure and love of ease grows. Envy and
"keeping up with the Joneses" make a wide breach in the wall of
Love's domain, the family, and allow pride, the final enemy of
God, to enter in!

Now Satan turns his baleful eye on obedience, which, in the
atmosphere he has succeeded in creating, is a languishing flower
growing in semi-darkness. Where sacrifice is absent, obedience
slowly dies. To kill it, to annihilate it, is now the next major
move of the prince of darkness, for which he laid the ground
work well.

Obedience is the essence of love, the essence of Christ, who
was obedient unto the death of the cross. He was obedient
because he loved, because he was Love Incarnate. Every
vocation, every call of God to a definite state of life, must be
given back to him wrapped in the beautiful garments of
obedience, which is better than sacrifice, but which takes its
strength from love, and brings forth the fruits of sacrifice.
Matrimony is truly the vocation to obedience! It is the natural
and supernatural school of obedience.

The family is a little church. It is also the primary
indissoluble unit of society. Its soul is in the hands of God. Its
heart and mind and way of life shape the heart and mind and way
of life of the nation. What the family is, that the nation will be.

Do we see the obedient wife, subject to her husband as God
meant her to be? Do we see the husband who sacrifices himself
for his wife, even as Christ sacrificed himself for his bride, the

Church? Do we see the obedient children, who see in their father what he truly is—Christ—and in the mother what she truly is—the Church? (See Eph 5:21-6:1.) Do we see those children? How many of them are there in our fair land?

It takes much sacrifice and love to teach children obedience. Perhaps it takes more to practice it. Yet, unless parents begin to live obedience, and to teach it to their offspring, we shall soon enter new catacombs.

Alone, a slender woman wrapped in eternal silence, Mary, the Mother of his Son, beseeches us—the children of her love, and of the earth she came from, the earth her Son once trod—to arise from our stupor, our selfishness, our love of ease and comfort, our hunger for the tinsel of passing things, and to begin to live in utter obedience to the laws of love which are the laws of God! She asks us for lives steeped in sacrifice, rooted in our answering song of love of God and his ways and order.

We turn deaf ears and go on our un-merry way, unable or unwilling, or both, to enter the austerely beautiful path of obedience and sacrifice, discipline and order. Oh! If only we knew what beauty awaits us around the bend of that road, for there Love will meet us, strewing our path with beauty undreamed of, teaching us to sing our love back to God, the God of love, who died for the love of us. If only husbands and wives understood the utter joy, order, happiness, and peace which would enter their lives, their homes, their hearts and those of their children!

Lent is a good time to begin to sing our human song of love back to God. It is the school of love, the school of that chant which alone has the power to restore each of us and our wounded world to the infinite peace of God. And that is a peace that no one can take away from us!

Chapter 20

Lent and the Mass

When the season of Lent comes, it brings with it Calvary. No matter how immersed in day-to-day living we may be, it is hard to escape a sort of inner realization that there *is* something different about these weeks. Many try to forget Calvary and all that it means, and to brush Lent out of their lives, but most of us pause inwardly and try to take stock of things that truly matter. How much this hurts only the individual knows.

Yet Lent, in a strange way, is a joyous season. For it is the completion of Christ's birth in his crib, that led slowly to the cross and brought us salvation and the Mass and sacraments. If only we turn to the cross, our lives will be renewed, as will our spiritual youth, and we will enter Easter with great joy. We will know that all things henceforth can be borne by each of us, if we live from Mass to Mass, preferably in twenty-four hour stretches!

For the Mass is the very breath of our spiritual life. There we are, face to face with the Lord of Hosts. There we become one with him. Then, refreshed and strengthened beyond our understanding, we once more can face whatever the day may bring. In the Mass we find Bread and Wine for the soul. We find Love bending down to us, Love lifting us, ever higher, to himself, until all things are right and well with us. For we have our being in him already on this earth. The Mass is the sum total of all our prayer life! Vocal: "With my voice I praise you." Mental: "My mind is slowly absorbed in his, and I begin to see, to understand." Contemplative: When we are unable to speak or think, we just "rest" in him.

All things come together in the Mass, for humanity comes together with God, and in God all things have their being. The Mass is a mighty bridge which brings the entire Church—living on earth now and those gone on to eternal life—together in an unbreakable unity. In doing so, it brings us peace, strength, and joy. For in the Mass we realize as through a glass darkly, that there is no loss of our Beloved, that we are not alone, that we walk in a goodly company of saints and martyrs. Life changes utterly and begins to make true sense to us when we participate in Mass daily. Our horizons become wider than all the universe, for they span time and eternity. Love grows within our soul until finally its eyes see Christ in all. Slowly, but oh, how surely, our whole person turns to God! Then the spirit of the evangelical counsels—of poverty, chastity, and obedience—of the Beatitudes and the Ten Commandments becomes simple and clear. We become free. How free cannot be told; it has to be experienced.

Lent is the commemoration of the passion of Christ, a book of great beauty for those who take time to read it. Lent is a song of love, with the Mass of the day its theme. Slowly, it unfolds its music, its pages filled with Christ's love for us.

To be so loved calls for loving back. If only we began that "loving back," our lives and those of our families, our nation, and all the world, would be changed and become Christ-centered instead of self-centered. The essence of it all can be found so easily, in any parish church, morning, noon, or night at Mass. A few minutes in a quiet church, following and participating in the Mass, preparing with the priest to offer the Perfect Sacrifice, and with it, our lives, our loves, our problems, our business, we plunge into the fire of the Mass—*God*—and come out ourselves a fire, a light, a flame, warming our cold world, lighting its path home.

Lent brings with it Calvary. Let us, then, arise and walk every step of these Lenten days until, standing with Mary under Christ's cross, we begin to love him back as he should be loved, and by that very loving, restore his kingdom to him. Our walking through the slow, beautiful days of Lent must begin with the Mass, the fruit of Calvary, the fruit of the Cross.

Chapter 21

Holy Week

Holy Week: the week before Easter. The Song of Songs, the song of divine love that is Lent, moves along and now becomes a throbbing, passionate outpouring of Love Incarnate dying for the redemption of his beloved, the soul of man! With an unbearable crescendo, its notes penetrate the hearts of those who love in return.

The Last Supper begins this penetration. For who but Love Incarnate would have such supreme ingenuity of love as to make himself sacrifice and sacrament, giving the cold world the Mass! His sea of fire, his sea of love, his school of love—to be warmed in, to be loved in, to learn to love Love in return, to feed on love! Oh wonder supreme—that same delicate ingenuity of love made him give himself as food and drink for his beloved, the soul of man!

Gethsemane: the notes of the supreme song of love mount higher. Their melody is poignant and beyond the deepest depth, like him who sings it. The notes penetrate the hearts of those who listen, penetrate like a fine sword of pain and longing.

In that desolate garden of Gethsemane, Love who is God bends and takes from his beloved first, the immense weight of original sin, then all sins, all the darkness that the soul has walked in, all its endless searchings, its shed and unshed tears, and—O miracle of love!—covers his own incomprehensible sinlessness, his white immaculateness, with the heavy, crushing, stinking mantle of them all.

Then, bathed in his own Precious Blood, he lifts the burden—the shame of it, the effort of it—and bears it to his Father! A spotless victim covered with *our* sins! All this is done because of his passionate love of us!

The Way of the Cross: step by step now, "station" after "station." How many of them were there truly? No one knows, nor does it matter. All that matters is that Love Supreme, Love Uncreated, Love Incarnate was unjustly condemned for love of us. Flagellated for love of us, he bore the heavy, rough, green-wood cross for us. He fell and bit the dry, hot dust of the road for us, then, on that rough cross, he laid himself down, with joy inexpressible. That is the true folly of love, a folly on the tree of pain, upon which he allowed himself to be nailed!

His song of songs, almost complete now, comes to one note, the note of exultant joy that, blending with infinite pain, expresses all that love is, and, in doing so, pierces heaven and earth for eternity with its divine voice!

Good Friday: Now Love is lifted up! It hangs from the tree. Its song of love descends upon the multitudes, a low, barely audible dirge of pain, which still contains a passionate, incredible declaration of love supreme, dying while the final note of that most sublime of all symphonies (that began with the cry of a baby born in a manger) trembles in the air. "It is consummated" (Jn 19:30)—a note no one was ever able to transcribe into earthly music, except into the notes of individual lives.

Now behold! Love is dead—for love's sake—to teach men that no greater love exists than to die for the beloved!

Such, then, is Holy Week. It is the one week of every calendar year in which every Catholic family will find the very essence of its vocation to love—its heart, its soul!

For this, God called them to their holy vocation of matrimony. Their Holy Week begins the moment they descend from the altar of God, after their nuptial Mass, before which they pledge themselves to one another for life, and to God for eternity. It is the first note of their answering song of love of Him, a note that grows into a symphony of surpassing beauty on their wedding night when they become, under the eyes of God, one flesh, one soul, one mind.

Henceforth, they will partake of the Last Supper, both by being present at the sacrifice of the holy Mass—the eternally-renewed sacrifice of Love on Calvary—at which they will be nourished with the Body and Blood of the same Love who is God, who, devising this ingenuity of love, died for love of them. They also will be "eaten up" themselves, for they must "feed" with their very substance each other and their children, giving lavishly, never counting the cost any more than he did. It is from God and their own substance that each of them, and their children, will grow in wisdom and grace before his face.

Gethsemane: Look, it is the same lonely garden—but now it is a garden of wedded life and wedded love. It is a garden to which each spouse must travel alone in the dark of the spiritual nights. Indeed, it is a garden enclosed, where, God alone knows how often one has taken on the burdens of the sorrows, misunderstandings, problems, and even sins of spouse and children.

For such is the inner meaning of that tremendous and holy word "vocation" that is never entered for oneself alone, but always, in the final end, for the common good of all the members of the Church. Especially is this true of the "little Church of God," which is the family, the members of which must so love one another that they must be ready to enter Gethsemane always. And there, in bloody sweat—symbolically speaking—they lift each other's burdens to the all-understanding and infinite mercy of God. May the Christ of the first Gethsemane then be at their sides!

The Way of the Cross: This is the way of life for each Catholic individually, the only way that leads to Calvary and Easter, the supreme path to heaven here on earth. Who of us mortals has not his or her *via crucis* to travel? Priests? Nuns? Single people living in the world? All must walk it. All must carry the cross God allotted them. But the family—husband and wife—from the very first day of their married life, begin their march. The Way of the Cross is the way of immolation, and that immolation, that dying to self, is the very heart of their married vocation!

Love serves. Love dies a thousand deaths and lives again for the beloved. How else can married love be sanctified, but by walking slowly, lovingly, each step of that steep way of Christ's Passion? Even in the natural order, in our poor, human language, fatherhood and motherhood are synonymous with unselfishness, with a love that has crucified itself for others.

Good Friday: This day comes to every family, sometimes unexpectedly, in death and losses. The eventide of life comes too, when husband and wife behold their task accomplished, their children reared and out of the family nest. So, when they see the beautiful face of death, they can say, "It is consummated—we have loved passionately, utterly, unto complete death to self."

With these words, which form the best account of the stewardship of our vocation, they may enter the joy of the Beatific Vision, which is the vision of the God who died for love of them on the one and only Good Friday, that day that heard his ultimate song of love. Now they, in turn, can sing their song of love for him, can sing it back to him for all eternity!

Chapter 22

Easter

Alleluia! Alleluia! The Lord is risen! Alleluia! The Feast of Feasts has come! The work of salvation is accomplished! The fault of Adam is atoned for, repaired, and the soul of each of his children is free again to come and dwell in the paradise for which it was created and which was created for it! Love, who is God, did all this for the soul of man—out of love!

Indeed Easter is the greatest feast of all, the feast of Love triumphant, of Christ who so loved us that even though he arose from the dead and ascended to his Father remains with us until the end of time in the Eucharist, the Blessed Sacrament of his love. He is here with his bride, the Church, which guides and nourishes us with his truths and himself.

Easter reminds us of all this outpouring of divine Love! No wonder that it is the feast of Love par excellence, the feast of the perfection of Charity who is God! It is a feast that holds within itself a lifetime of lessons about love. It should be the school of our vocation to love. All Catholics are called to it. For this we were born on this earth—to learn to love God, and to prove our love to him, by loving our neighbor.

All Catholics should enter this school, but the Catholic family should remain there always. For even as they participate in the feasts of the Church, there is a "form," a "grade" for each feast. Easter should become a sort of "postgraduate course" of studies in that all-important curriculum.

The family has a tangible vocation to love. It is by falling in love that men and women hear the call of God to that hardest of all vocations, holy matrimony. God, knowing full well how difficult is their "course," gives them to each other, so that each may help the other, and together, they may help their children to fulfil his commandments: to love him above all things, and to love their neighbors as themselves. How much must go into that simple directive! First, seeing Christ in each other, they will have to love each other with a great love. It will be a love of service and sacrifice, given joyfully, instantly, at all times, hard and easy. This will demand humility, the fertile soil of their souls, that must be cultivated constantly in order to grow the tremendous virtues of faith, hope, and charity. For without them, their marriage will wither before it has time to bring forth its first bud.

Faith, hope, and charity are reached in their perfection by the austere and beautiful virtue of obedience. This means obedience to the laws of God in general, and obedience to the laws of God as they so very specially apply to the married vocation.

Consider how much faith must go into just having children, as God sends them, in our modern times, with its shortage of housing and its whole inimical attitude toward large families!

How powerful must be their hope, that holds on against all odds to the substance of things unseen, while the substance of things seen, heard, and touched draws husband and wife with a powerful current against that very virtue, and whispers constantly, in a beguiling, tragic whisper close to despair that the life demanded by their holy vocation is too hard, that they can and should compromise, be it even a little, that, after all, heaven and God are far away, and today is today, and the line of least resistance will do.

As to charity, the mother of all virtues, where they come to rest and full flowering, how infinite must be the *caritas*, the love, the charity of the family! For, in truth, it is the school of charity. That is where love must be taught in its fullness. That is where it first clothes itself in the flesh of the Word who is

God—touchable, visible to the children, in the love that mother and father have for each other. In the unselfishness of that love, in the spilling of it, by both, in constant service to one another, their children, and their neighbors, there are laid the wider foundations of charity, where husband, wife, and children learn to love God as he should be loved, utterly and passionately, and to love their neighbor for his sake.

How quickly the great tranquility of God's order would be established in our fair land if Christian parents understood this! There would be no need to restore justice. For in that school of love, the family would learn that all men and women are their brothers and sisters in Christ—Blacks, Jews, "foreigners," and all those now considered second-class citizens. All would become one in love, if children were taught, as they should be from the very beginning of their lives, to see the most beautiful face in the world—the face of Christ—in each neighbor.

How quickly happiness, true and real, would make her home in the homes of our land if parents and children learned, in the bosom of their own families, that the Commandments, the Beatitudes, and the counsels of perfection were their way to the perfection which Christ wants all men and woman to achieve. All this would be theirs if they embraced obedience, and brought this vital virtue to live with them unto the end of their days. For it would lead them, by the shortest route, to the very heart of Christ, who was obedient unto death!

> Give way to one another in obedience to Christ. Wives should regard their husbands as they regard the Lord, since as Christ is head of the Church and saves the whole body, so is the husband the head of his wife, and as the Church submits to Christ, so should wives to their husbands, in everything. Husbands should love their wives just as Christ loved the Church and sacrificed himself for her.... In the same way, husbands must love their wives as they love their own bodies.... Each one of you must love his wife as he loves himself; and let every wife respect her husband.

Children, be obedient to your parents in the Lord
—that is your duty (Eph 5:21-25, 28, 33-6:1).

A husband, the Christ of the little church of the Catholic
family, obedient to all the laws of God and to his glorious
vocation; a wife obedient to her husband (for isn't she the Church
to his Christhood?) and children obedient to their parents. Oh, the
joyous freedom that would come to such a family, the true
freedom of the children of God! How almost overnight our sick
world would heal!

It is against obedience that Satan today pin-points all his
attacks. How well he knows that if he breaks up the heart of the
nation, the unit of society, the "little church" of Christ, the
family, he will succeed in leading us on the first step to utter
chaos and put our feet on the first rung of the downward ladder
to the catacombs, actual and spiritual, that our tragic world is
already facing.

Great intelligence that Satan is, he knows that if he can
break down the divinely established hierarchy of authority of
husband and wife, and through them sow disobedience and lack
of respect for parental authority in the children, he will have
sown the seeds of a future and complete breakdown of society.
Father and mother will be under the unholy guidance of Satan
himself on the hallowed ground of the family. Where
disobedience abides, Christ cannot live, for it is the poisonous
fruit of pride and the mother of many sins.

Easter is the feast of living, glorious Love, who walks
among us until the end of time and who reigns in heaven, without
beginning or end, waiting for us to enjoy it for eternity, if only
we make the lessons of its "school of love" our own during our
short exile on this earth.

Let us begin, those of us who have been called so very
specially to marriage, the vocation to love, to establish millions
of "little churches" of God, millions of truly Christian families
whose only aim in life is to become saints of God, lovers of God,
by truly making their family life a school of love!

Alleluia! Christ is risen! Alleluia! Truly he is risen! May we
too rise with him! Alleluia!

Chapter 23

Ascension

Jesus returned to his Father in heaven forty days after his Resurrection. We celebrate this on the feast of the Ascension.

He had shown himself alive to them after his Passion by many demonstrations: for forty days he had continued to appear to them and tell them about the kingdom of God....

He was lifted up while they looked on, and a cloud took him from their sight (Acts 1:3, 9).

Let us make the glorious feast of Christ's Ascension our own, we who are married and who need to understand in these barren, soulless days of our sterile century the blinding joy of our faith that rests in the very essence of glory—God.

Let us steep ourselves in the memory, the "sight" of the Ascension as given by the Gospel witnesses of that incredible day. They had known Christ well and had witnessed his public life. There were among them some who knew his early and private life well too. All of them knew of his trial, passion, and ignominious death on the cross. They had seen his burial place, except Judas, who was dead. They had seen him after his resurrection, and now they saw his ascension. Slowly, slowly, majestic in his glorified human body, up ... up ... into the heights of heaven he went.

114

The pattern is there for us to see. Our love also "incarnated itself" and became palpable, reflecting itself in our human words, glances, touches. Then our human love was lifted up to a sacrament, the sacrament of Matrimony, where we became one in flesh, in a unity that, in time, would yield its fruit—living, breathing children, flesh of our flesh, yet incarnations of our love too.

From the steps of the altar where our love becomes a sacrament, we enter Nazareth and the hidden life of our Lord, for isn't that the pattern followed by millions of married couples? After the little flurry among the few who know of their engagement and wedding, they seem to nearly disappear into the immense, anonymous mass of mankind. They go to live wherever their state of life calls them to live, unknown and un-heralded, living simply, even hiddenly, as far as the big stream of humanity is concerned.

Not for the likes of us are fame and notoriety, the splash of splendor. No. For us there is ordinariness, a sameness that becomes almost monotony, at least outwardly. Love, sickness, birth, and death in such families make only little ripples as far as the big, outside world is concerned. But oh! The slow growth of forthcoming glory that goes on behind the doors of a thousand homes that look to the passers-by so alike in their seemingly drab sameness!

Slowly, out of wedded love, so well hidden in the modern Nazareths of life, virtues grow. Humility takes root. Unselfish-ness brings forth its fragrant flowers. Thoughtfulness for one another designs a border for the enclosed garden of the Lord. Roses of charity varied in color grow in the fertile soil of wedded love. Faith, hand in hand with hope, fertilizes the soil and waters it when the droughts of life hit it again and again. Yes, that is what is really happening, though it may seem monotonous to many.

Remember, though, that Nazareth led to Christ's public life. Each couple and their children must enter a "public life," according to their holy vocation. Just by *being* a Christian family, by living their hidden life well, they will witness to the Father, for they will slowly be clothed with Christ, and make him visible to all who in any way touch their family life in the market places of the world where such families have their being.

They will preach too. Silently, by living their faith to the hilt always. Articulately, by opening their mouths in the utter simplicity of love, when it is called for, and witnessing in words according to their knowledge and talents to God and the things of God.

Small is their voice. Small, too, may be the public arena God allotted to them. But then, small is a little pebble thrown in a lake—but watch the eddies from its fall grow and grow until the biggest touches the shores many miles away. Such pebbles thrown into the lake of the world are true Christian families who witness in their life and speech, day in and day out, to the Lord their God! Such, then, will be the following of Christ's footsteps by a Catholic family. A hidden life, a public life, and of course his passion and death.

Temptation, darkness, bewilderment—all will come and dwell with them. They will go through Gethsemane. They must. It was his way, and so it will be theirs. Like him, they will cry out in anguish, but all will be well with them if, like him, they always add, "Not my will but thine be done in me" (Mt 26:39).

Cruel men will come, or cruel days, that may send them one by one through their flagellation, their crowning with thorns, their way of the cross, and finally their crucifixion. Yes, it may be cruel men, it may be death, sickness, sorrow of a thousand kinds and with a thousand faces. It will inevitably come, because individually and collectively the family must relive, as all Catholics must, Christ's life on earth, to reach their Easter.

If they do it with grace, joy, and love, they too will know the fullness of the glory of Ascension, when finally the day will come when God will send his messenger of love and call them to his embrace. Then the feast of the Ascension will be reproduced in them. Freed from the body, the soul will rise—glorious in the sight of angels and God—into his waiting arms. Later, "on the last day," the soul will know once more the touch of flesh, glorified this time, as Christ's was! (1 Thes 4:16; 1 Cor 15:42-3) But the waiting for it will be but an instant as men reckon time, for who thinks of waiting when one is existing in the very heart of Love, who is God?

Yes, let us married folks make the feast of the Ascension our very own, because if we do, we shall so live, husband, wife, and children, as to make ready for its breath-taking golden glory.

Chapter 24

Pentecost

When Pentecost day came round, they had all met in one room, when suddenly they heard what sounded like a powerful wind from heaven, the noise of which filled the entire house in which they were sitting; and something appeared to them that seemed like tongues of fire; these separated and came to rest on the head of each of them. They were all filled with the Holy Spirit, and began to speak foreign languages as the Spirit gave them the gift of speech (Acts 2:1-4).

This is the feast of the Holy Spirit. In many countries it is called the feast of the Crimson Dove, who on that day so long ago shed a few feathers of his wings, the spread of which covers the earth. These first few feathers plummeted down, down, into an Upper Room, and touched the crown of the heads of a few of the disciples bowed down before the sound of the mighty wind which the feathers made as they came in.

The feathers were tongues of fire to them, full of fecundity—for on that day the bride of Christ was born, the Catholic Church, the visible whole which we call the Mystical Body of Christ. Gifts poured that day upon the disciples in that upper room—courage beyond the courage of men descended on them. Faith was knighted. Love became all-consuming, in a fire which they could not contain but had to rush out and share right there on the streets, with any who had ears to hear! That was the first Pentecost!

Pentecost repeats itself, from that day until the end of time. It repeats itself, for two feathers from the immense wings of the Crimson Dove fall daily, hourly, on this dark earth, lighting its darkness with the fire of their descending and resting on the heads of two—a man and a woman! True marriage is a little Pentecost (if Pentecost can ever be called "little"). For behold: Here are two human beings consumed with love! Love that came to them through the Crimson Dove—a call of God, a vocation to love him in a certain manner and a certain way. He made that call a most holy one, for he raised it to the heights of a sacrament of august and poignant beauty. The two called to this vocation most assuredly need the gifts of faith, courage, and light, for their way to God is through many dark nights!

These two will also have to pray in their upper room through all their courtship to be very sure that this is the road, and this is the way in which they best can serve, love, and adore the God who made them just for this, so that they may know him in eternal bliss. How shall they know for certain, unless through the gentle touch of the red feathers that fall with such consummate grace down, down from the wings of the Crimson Dove that alone can confirm them in their love, and lift it up—up into the very heart of the God who is Love!

Here they are. Behold them now—two who kneel on the altar steps, two who pledge to love, cherish and live their whole life this vocation to love their Triune God through each other. Yes, here they are—two touched lightly by crimson feathers that are not feathers at all, but the fire of the Holy Spirit descending on them in their Pentecost!

Behold them: two coming down the altar steps; two becoming one in the flesh; two becoming one in soul, mind, and love within the flaming light of the Crimson Dove; two unable to contain overflowing love, rushing out of themselves and then coming back, holding in their arms the fruit of their love and its flame—a child—then two, three, and more. Lo! Behold now they are themselves a family, a little church, their lives lived out in Pentecost. The feast of the Dove, the feast of the Fire of Love begotten by the Father and Son, loving each other in a strange and eternal fecundity of love.

Yes, the feast of Pentecost is indeed the feast of the Fire of Love come to rest on the earth to renew its face. Yet it seems as if the Crimson Dove loves especially to nestle in the heart of the little churches which are the families that make up the big Church.

And Mary, the Mother of Fair Love, knows the secrets of all Pentecosts, for she did not get feathers from its wings. She was overshadowed by him and the immense crimson wings of the Dove lifted her up in a flaming embrace in which she became the Spouse of Love. So it is fitting that she be there when her Spouse descends into human hearts. And it is fitting, too, for man and wife to bring her into the family, the little church of God, for if she reigns in it as queen, the Father, Son and Holy Spirit will dwell in it with a deep repose. Pentecost will indeed be a major family feast.

Chapter 25

St. John the Baptist: Family Fire
June 24

In the days of King Herod of Judaea there lived a priest called Zechariah ... and he had a wife, Elizabeth by name.... Both were worthy in the sight of God.... But they were childless: Elizabeth was barren and they were getting on in years.

Then there appeared to him [Zechariah] the angel of the Lord.... The angel said to him, "Zechariah, do not be afraid, your prayer has been heard. Your wife Elizabeth is to bear you a son and you must name him John...."

Mary set out ... and went as quickly as she could.... She went into Zechariah's house and greeted Elizabeth. Now as soon as Elizabeth heard Mary's greeting, the child leapt in her womb and Elizabeth was filled with the Holy Spirit. She gave a loud cry and said, "Of all women you are the most blessed, and blessed is the fruit of your womb.... For the moment your greeting reached my ears, the child in my womb leapt for joy" (Lk 1:5-7, 11, 13, 39-44).

What has the feast of St. John the Baptist to do with the family? The answer lies in the word fire. St. John was set on fire before he was born. Yes, set on fire by Christ, before Christ was

121

born. The fire was the fire of love. This is what happened when Mary went to visit her cousin Elizabeth. She was the first chalice, as it were, to carry Christ to men. Hidden in her womb then, as he is hidden in the Host today, he showed his divinity by setting afire the heart of an infant yet unborn. The same miracle is repeated again and again in our days.

People come to the great sacrament of the Holy Eucharist, many yet unborn to the fire of divine love. Oh, they have been baptized, to be sure, in the waters of baptism, even as Christ was baptized by John, but they are yet unawakened to their own capacities for divine love. Then, suddenly one day, they catch a glimpse of what it means to be a whole Christian, a completely integrated Catholic. They leap with joy in the womb of that inner vision.

Especially should this be the case with husband and wife. They have come together in that divine love— for what else is marital love but a facet, a gem from the crown of eternal uncreated Love in whom all true loves meet?

St. John the Baptist was the anchorite, the dweller in deserts, the man who made straight the paths of the Lord, the precursor, the martyr! He should be the patron saint of married folks. Let us dwell a little on the reason for this statement, which at first may strike you as illogical, for it would seem that this virgin man, far removed from marriage, would be the last to become its patron. Yet, the bridge word here is *fire*.

It was the fire of love that made St. John leap in the womb of his mother at the approach of Christ. It is the fire of love that makes people "leap," forsaking mother and father and cleaving to one another. From whence did that "fire of love" come to them, ordinary men and women that they are? It came from the same Christ who called them to their sublime vocation to love. It was the fire of love that drove St. John the Baptist into the desert to prepare himself for the immense task of being a precursor of the Lord of Hosts, to be able "to make straight the way of the Lord" (Mk 1:3). And what is marriage but the dwelling of a man and a woman together in a desert? They are two against the world, yet in the midst of the world, a world which is indeed a desert the like of which St. John never faced.

How infinite will be the mortifications and penances of the husband and wife if they are to persevere in their marital and Christian integrity, if they are to make straight the ways of the Lord in their hearts and souls, and in those of their children! How slow and thorough will be their "inner fast of herbs and locusts," how bittersweet their days, how full of "watches and prayers" their nights!

Marriage, for all its intoxicating natural and supernatural beauty, is in the natural order the hardest vocation of all. Yes, St. John the Baptist should be its patron. He should bring to it his fire of the love of God, and show how it can burn brightly, so brightly that it will illuminate not only the little church that is every Catholic home (or should be) but also the big Church, the Mystical Body of Christ, his beloved Bride.

No wonder the saint's feast day is celebrated in many countries with bonfires. No wonder the Church gave the world a blessing on that bonfire. Fire is the watchword of St. John. Fire is the soul of St. John, and the same fire must be the very soul of a family.

St. John spoke the truth fearlessly and paid for it with his life. St. John preached repentance constantly, in season and out, and so must the Catholic family. They, like St. John, must speak and live the *full truth of God,* just as fearlessly as St. John did. What our sick and dying world needs is just such families, families that clothe their lives, day in and day out, with the flesh of the Word that dwells among us.

Make no mistake, it is *heroic* to do this in the second part of the twentieth century and beyond, and it will make straight the paths of the Lord to thousands of other families who are just waiting to be shown how to walk in "straight and narrow paths."

Oh, it may cost the Catholic family a great price to take St. John the Baptist for its patron. Father, perhaps, is not going to be president of a vast concern. Money will not be over-plentiful, as people reckon such a commodity today. There will be no millions to figure taxes on. Mother will not have that wonderful house, with all the servants worldly women dream about and nag their husbands for. The Joneses will be left all to themselves and no one will try "to keep up with them." Junior may not go to college, but do an honest day's work as a plumber or carpenter. Sis will not belong to the Junior League, nor have a "debut in society."

But under St. John's patronage, such a family will be wealthy in the joy and peace that transcend all human understanding. They will be rich in the love of God and one another, so rich that they will be able to give of their wealth of love to any who knock at their door hungry and thirsty for it!

They will be apostles of the market place, with whom many will wish to "keep up." They will be what their patron saint is—fire on earth. They will be little fires that, spreading, will set the world aflame for God; and hence make straight his paths in the souls of many.

They will seemingly, like St. John, lose their lives for the love of Christ and, even as he, they will lose their heads, or so people will say. (For anyone in love with God appears foolish in the eyes of the world.) Yet they will gain a kingdom, and they will lay up unto themselves treasures neither moth nor thief can get at.

It is St. John, again, who will teach the husband and the wife to find God in the hard martyr-like discipline of their holy vocation, in the desert of pain and sorrow that comes to each human family. It will be he who will straighten their wills against the winds of temptation which rock the lovely house of love each marriage is. It will be his ways that will show them their way, when, worried and a little lost, they stand at some crossroads that marriage inevitably leads to.

He it is, too, past master at mastering himself, who will teach them obedience to God's will and commands, his beatitudes and counsels, which each family must make their own according to their married state, or perish from spiritual malnutrition.

This applies equally to father and mother and children. St. John, by instructing parents in the ways of the Lord, will help to instruct the fruits of their beautiful love, their children, to walk in the same straight, narrow ways.

Yes, St. John the Baptist should be a patron saint of families, for, fire of Love that he is, he should begin to make straight these important ways of the Lord. If there is one part of humanity that must become "straight," it is our modern Catholic family that lives in these strange times betwixt and between the heaven of their faith and the hell that is the modern world, so full of secularism, materialism, paganism, and all the "isms" except true Catholicism!

St. John the Baptist, come, and make the foundation of our crumbling society straight and firm! Save the soul of the world, by saving the family. Amen.

Chapter 26

Saints Peter and Paul, Patrons of Married Life: June 29

This is the feast of the mid-year, falling on June 29, during the month of the Sacred Heart. It is a great feast, prepared for in the old days by a week's fast, abstinence, prayer, and mortification. Truly, all these are needed to celebrate with joyous understanding the feast of St. Peter, the rock and the keeper of the keys, and the feast of St. Paul, the Apostle to the Gentiles, the apostle of love.

On this continent of North America in our day this glorious feast passes almost unnoticed. Even its vigil is barely kept, except in some monasteries or convents of strict observance. Yet the Apostles are the first fruits of God's Incarnation. It is to Peter he gave the keys of the kingdom. It is on him he built his Church: "You are Peter and on this rock I will build my Church. ... I will give you the keys of the kingdom of heaven ... " (Mt 16:18-19). And Paul, his first own convert after the Resurrection! Spectacular! Miraculous! Fantastic! Stupendous!

Oh, many were the converts of Christ in those early, blessed days when the Apostles and disciples still lived, remembering the color of his eyes, the sound of his living voice, the warm touch of his hands. He spoke to St. Paul, however, only after his Death, Resurrection, and Ascension: "Paul, Paul, why are you persecuting me?" (Acts 9:4), thus recalling for us the one yardstick of judgment that he had given in the Gospel: "Whatsoever you do to the least of my brothers, you do to me"

(Mt 25:40). His words merged everyone with Christ, and Christ with everyone. In persecuting Christians, Paul was persecuting Christ. This was Christ expounding the doctrine of his Mystical Body, the Church, identifying himself utterly with his beloved. Our love of neighbor is the only proof of our love of God.

Oh, the simplicity of God! It is complex only to those whose eyes are sealed and ears held. There it is, in black and white, for all to hear and see.

First, the fruit of the Incarnation, the new commandment made clear, the brotherhood of all men and women in Christ, under the Fatherhood of God, bought at the price of Incarnation and Redemption. Then, the utter identification of Christ with his Church, his Bride, in the burning flame of love.

Indeed, the feast of Saints Peter and Paul on June 29 is the feast of love's eternal ingenuity, its eternal ability to speak in accents always new! It is a great feast indeed, but what has it to do with holy matrimony, that sublime and hard vocation that has to be lived day by day, by a man and a woman and their children who are in the world, but not of it? Let us see.

First, consider Peter, the rock, the keeper of the keys of the kingdom. Peter was married before he met Christ and later, in Christ, the Church became his spouse. He is a prototype of all husbands, for he is Christ's representative to us, vicar of the Crucified, yet a human husband and head of the "little church" of the family first.

Right indeed! For wife and children, authority, safety, security—all rooted in love, all coming directly from the very hands of God in the most holy sacrament of Matrimony—are centered in the husband.

So let husbands place themselves under the patronage of Peter. He, the fisherman, will teach them how to love through all the storms of the sea of life. He, who betrayed Christ, will teach them how to weep, when in their frailty, they fail and fall. He, who was forgiven, will impart to them the secret of God's grace and mercy, and tell them how it heals and makes whole again, and gives ever more strength for the immense natural and supernatural task of protecting, cherishing, nourishing and lifting up the "little church"—the family entrusted to them.

St. Peter will also teach them how to die to self and live in God in their vocation, and see grace come to every member of the family through that death to self of its head. To whom could a husband and father turn for better guidance of his barque on the stormy sea of life, than to a fisherman who knows the sea, and once even walked upon it?

Consider Paul, the Apostle to the Gentiles. He is the inspiration and guide to husband and wife to become apostles to the modern "Gentiles" in the market place of our world today. O tent maker Paul, teach us married folks how to make the "tent" of our home secure against the tearing claws of Satan, who constantly goes about around it like a roaring lion seeking whom he may devour (1 Pt 5:8).

St. Paul is the apostle of charity, whose love-poem to charity in chapter 13 of his first letter to the Corinthians has never been surpassed by mortal man. Yes, St. Paul will teach us who are wedded in love how to love God and each other passionately, utterly, in complete surrender.

Teach us how to make ours a house of love, where God dwells and where Mary makes her home, a place where the fruits of our wedded love—children—are lifted up to dwell from birth to death in the arms of God, from whom all love stems. You, Paul, tent maker who were lifted up unto the seventh heaven, come and make your abode with us, as you did in days of old with so many married folks. Teach us to make our house a heaven for all who enter and for all who dwell therein.

Yes, Peter and Paul, whose feast falls in the month of June, the month of the Sacred Heart, the month of Love all-encompassing, the month of weddings, we about to marry and we already in that holy state, invite you to come and dwell with us, for we have great need of you, we who in our humble, small fashion are "little churches" of the God of Love! We promise to celebrate your feast day with reverence and joy, for indeed you belong so specially to us married folks too!

Chapter 27

The Assumption of Our Lady August 15

The Most Blessed Virgin Mary, when the course of her earthly life was completed, was taken up body and soul into the glory of heaven, where she already shares in the glory of her Son's Resurrection, anticipating the resurrection of all members of his Body *(Catechism of the Catholic Church,* § 974).

August, the month of fruitfulness, of harvest, is indeed a fitting setting for this glorious feast of Our Lady—her Assumption, her homecoming, after a long exile, to heaven, to her Son, his Father, and the Holy Spirit, her Spouse. What a joyous feast it is!

One can almost feel its throbbing song of gladness! When did her Son come to bring her into her full queenship? Was it early, at dawn, when the sun, like a shy lover, arises softly to catch the first look at his beloved, the earth, while she is still half-asleep, half-awake? Was it at eventide, when the sun, reluctantly bidding her farewell, bedecked her in the beauty of all his golden raiment and showered on her the gems of his own setting? Or was it in the soft, starlit night, become resplendently white for the second time in her existence, with choirs of angels, principalities, and powers filling its depths with glories, this time unheard by shepherds, or any other human ears?

It matters not. What matters is that he came and took her, his immaculate Virgin Mother unto his eternal kingdom and glory, to reign there as Queen of Heaven and Earth. It must have been a moment of ineffable beauty, of joy untranslatable into human words, a moment of gladness that shook worlds and spheres, an instant of divine love meeting a human love, a love divinized, refined, fused, melted into the triune love of Father, Son, and Holy Spirit.

She must have stood there resplendent, the woman clothed with silence, in the very center of the love of Father and Son, under the outspread wings of the Holy Spirit, the Crimson Dove. Yes, she stood there, the only creature of earth thus exalted, the mother, the channel, of all graces.

Yes, the feast of Mary's Assumption into heaven is one of the glories of the Church. It is also, or should be, a feast of the family. For it is the final celebration of two yeses—both of which must belong to the "little church," the Catholic family. They must make up its very foundations, and be mortar to its house to make it secure against the foe, for the foe ever roars like a lion around it, seeking to devour it.

A slim little girl of fifteen heard the mighty angel Gabriel tell her, "Hail, full of grace!" and explain that she would be overshadowed by the Most High, and would bear a son, the Son of God, in her virginal womb. Having delivered his message, the angel waited, waited for her answer. So did a hushed, amazed heaven. So did the universe of space and spheres. The redemption of all humanity hung on the answer of a woman barely fifteen! Then came her "yes," spoken with the soft voice of youth, yet loud enough to pierce all centuries and make us wish to spill our life at her feet in gratitude for it! "Let what you have said be done to me" (Lk 1:38).

How many millions of women since have repeated this yes, in how many accents, in how many tongues? For what is the "yes" of a young woman to a man proposing to her, but an echo of Mary's yes? For what she is saying "yes" to is nothing less than the reenacting of Mary's advent and of Christmas.

Married life is truly the school of sanctity where, with the birth of each child, Christ is born, not only in the child but also in the parents. Visibly, as it were, in flesh, and invisibly, yet palpably, in souls.

What is sanctity, marital or single, but our being pregnant with Christ and giving birth to Christ in us, and the bringing of Christ to full manhood in us, so that the world may see him in our lives! We must decrease and he increase, so that when the time of our dissolution and our soul's assumption is at hand, we may in truth say with St. Paul, "I live now, not I, but Christ lives in me" (Gal 2:20).

All Catholics are called to say that yes, but especially the husband and the wife. They have the additional grace not only to give birth to Christ in their souls but also to beget other Christs in the children of their flesh and love. Indeed, Mary's Assumption is a feast of married folks—their goal as it were, the crowning glory of their marital life, the feast that they should ever keep before their eyes, for it will be, in a manner of speaking, theirs if they, like she, make their lives a constant yes to God's will as expressed in their sublime state of life.

But what of the second yes of Mary, which must have taken place, unheard even by John the Beloved under the cross of her dying Son? She must have told it to no one but her Son.

St. John Eudes tells us that tradition has it that Jesus and Mary spoke together before his Passion, and that he must have told her then that she would have to stay on earth after he left, an exile of love, to mother his infant Church. Since her will was ever united to his, she must have spoken that unheard yes instantly, no matter what pain it might have caused her.

Who can probe, be it ever so reverently, the loneliness of Mary, left behind on earth? And who can fathom her joy at doing the will of her Beloved? He who dares to attempt such meditation will touch the ecstasy of her Assumption into heaven.

Yet, in those hidden, long years of exile, in that yes that comes to us through the writings of saints and tradition, lies also the whole road of the family, the "little church" on earth. Since the Ascension of her Son to heaven it is to Mary that each of us can turn for help and strength. For where is the husband, the wife, the children, who do not have to repeat that unheard yes of their heavenly Mother? Death, separation, exile from one another are but a thousand facets of the same Marian apostolate. The mothering of infants, be it the infant Church, as she had to do, or the infant child, or the infant Christ in the soul of husband and wife and children—all demand that oft-repeated yes to God's most holy will. All contain Mary's pain, Mary's sadness, Mary's joys, as she, with love and obedience inexpressible, lived on and on, doing the will of God, waiting for her exile to end.

Yes, Mary's two immense yeses, though belonging to all Christians, belong especially to truly Catholic families, who desire to love God madly, as she did, and who realize that such love demands nothing less than her yeses repeated again and again, like so many songs of love!

Chapter 28

October
Month of the Rosary

A crucifix ... A large bead ... three small beads ... a large bead ... a little space ... ten smaller beads ... a space ... ten smaller beads ... made out of anything ... strung on a cord or a chain. Repeat the pattern of one large and ten small beads five times, and you have the Catholic Rosary, which the Church considers so important a prayer that she dedicates a whole month of the year to it! Strange, that such a simple thing rates so high, but then, all things of God are simple. Saints also are simple, because *God* is simple.

Consider the Rosary. Yes, at first it appears to be just a string of beads, arranged in a specific, perhaps somewhat incomprehensible design. But look closer!

A crucifix, a cross, is its beginning and its end. Here we see the sign of our salvation, and a sign of contradiction to many. Here we see the answer to all our modern problems. On it we say the *Credo*, the Creed, our Christian, Catholic declaration of faith in an age of faithlessness.

Then we have a large bead for the Our Father, Christ's own prayer, which covers all the needs of men and women, that makes us his brothers and sisters, and brothers and sisters of one another, inviting us to call God the Father *our* Father too.

Three small beads: Three Hail Marys. The angelic salutation of Gabriel to Mary. "Hail Mary, full of grace. The Lord is with you!" (See Lk 1:28.) A reminder of her answer, her "yes" to God that brought about the Incarnation and our redemption, by bringing Jesus, the Son of God, and Mary, to our parched earth, to be born, to live and die, so that we might again enter the paradise Adam and Eve had lost, so that we might know the face of God and of Love. For through her yes, the Word took flesh and dwelt among us. "Let what you have said be done to me" (Lk 1:38).

Then a bead of glory. "Glory be to the Father, and to the Son, and to the Holy Spirit, as it was in the beginning, is now, and ever shall be, world without end!" For this we were created —to render glory to our Father, his Son, and the Holy Spirit.

Slowly, crucifix and beads slip through the fingers of babies, children, and young men and women of all states of life all over the world. Slowly, people everywhere repeat the prayers that hold within their familiar words the whole of the Catholic faith. Said thus, it would be already a beautiful prayer, a wonderful tribute to God and his Immaculate Mother, but it is more, oh so much more!

It is a pilgrimage of our minds, hearts, and souls into the deep mysteries of faith. It is a prayer of mind as well as lips. We meditate on the mysteries of our faith as they slowly, majestically, follow the pattern of the beads.

Monday the Joyful Mysteries of the Rosary open their song of gladness to eyes blessed by faith. Our meditation is on the Annunciation by the angel to Mary on the first decade of ten beads, on Mary's Visitation to Elizabeth on the second, on the Nativity of the Lord on the third, on his Presentation in the Temple on the fourth, and on the finding of Jesus in the Temple on the fifth.

Tuesday brings us to the price of our redemption, with the Sorrowful Mysteries—Christ's Agony in the Garden of Gethsemane, his Scourging at the Pillar, his Crowning with Thorns, his Carrying of the Cross, and his Death on the Cross.

Wednesday shows us the fruits of the Incarnation and Redemption. Here we see Christ's Resurrection, his Ascension, the Descent of the Holy Spirit upon the Apostles, the Assumption of the Blessed Virgin Mary into heaven, and her Crowning as Queen of Heaven and Earth.

Thursday we begin all over again with the joys of our faith. Friday we enter its sorrow. Saturday and Sunday we behold its glory.

A slender, simple thing, a rosary. But how infinitely deep, how all-embracing! How beautifully fitting for all who live on earth—the learned, the unlearned, and all in-between, the very young, the very old, and all ages between. It is, above all, the perfect prayer for the family. For, if they pray it together, they will indeed stay together.

The Rosary begins with a cross. It is on the cross that Incarnated Love proved to us his love for us. It is from that crucified Love that all true love is born. It is by its sign that it grows and flourishes. It is by embracing it that husband and wife are able to weather all the pains, problems, and difficulties of their sublime vocation. It is by its strength that they will overcome all temptations. For it is the tree of Love, and Christ who is love, its fruit. In him, through him, for him, they are wedded. From him they will receive all the graces needed for their state. In him, they will die to self and be reborn in glory. The daily rosary, family prayer par excellence, begins with the Cross and the Credo.

Hail Marys follow one another, tender and simple as the little maid of fifteen summers who became the Virgin Mother of God. Days follow days, as the family repeats the angelic salutation, and gently, Mary shows them herself as the shortcut to Christ, for he chose to come to humanity through her. How will we best go to him? Through her.

Slowly, wherever the Rosary is said, the beautiful Queen of the Rosary embraces husband, wife, and children. For she who is the mother of God is also the mother of humanity and the channel of all graces given by God to the Church. Can we doubt for an instant that where Mary is honored, Christ, his Father, and the Holy Spirit are absent? Who is there who can "unpetal" for us, one by one, the roses of the Joyful, Sorrowful, and Glorious Mysteries, flowers of our faith, better than Mary, who lived each one so fully, so completely?

Husband, wife, and children need to steep themselves in each mystery, for they are the warp and woof of their lives. Each Christian knows that he has to pass through the joyful ones to be able to take the sorrowful ones, and, through these, enjoy the glorious ones. Those who glorify God daily through the Glory Be will most assuredly glorify him in heaven.

A slender thing, the Rosary. Yet strong enough to be the way to God through Mary. Small enough to hide in the palm of a child's hand, yet big enough to be a school for saints, which every family must be. Simple enough to be said by babies, deep enough to give food for a life's meditation to sages—a holy prayer.

Yes, the Rosary is a family prayer. It will bring the tranquility of God's order to the foundation of our crumbling society, to the family, without which there is no restoring of the world to Christ. No wonder the Church dedicates a whole month of the calendar year to its sublime simplicity, its infinite depths. Let us who are so especially called to the vocation of love through marriage recite it daily, and make October truly the month of the Rosary.

Chapter 29

November, Month of the Holy Souls
Bypassing Purgatory

All who die in God's grace and friendship, but still imperfectly purified, are indeed assured of their eternal salvation; but after death they undergo purification, so as to achieve the holiness necessary to enter the joy of heaven.

The church gives the name *Purgatory* to this final purification of the elect (*Catechism of the Catholic Church*, § 1030-1031).

The Church dedicates the entire month of November to the souls in purgatory. Why a whole month? And why do we Catholics call them "the poor souls?" How can a soul assured of the golden, blinding glory of the Lord be poor? It can't. It is rich with joy, for it will see God. It is rich with pain, for now it knows fully what mortal sin is, what venial sin looks like, what faults and imperfections do to souls when the white light of God's justice falls upon them on their final judgement day.

They know too the price that was paid for those sins. And their pain, their waiting, is indeed rich with love of him who paid that price out of love for them! For they saw him face to face, and now they hunger for him with a hunger beyond all imaginable hunger, and that hunger makes up their pains.

137

The thirty short days that make up November are given to us to enrich the rich souls in purgatory. For in their immense wealth, they lack but one thing—the ability to shorten their exile from glory, from God. Unbelievable as this is, we whose souls are yet imprisoned in the clothing of flesh can give them—the rich ones, the sure ones—the alms of our prayers. We can give more. We can see to it that Masses are offered for their release! One Mass—how many souls does it set free to soar into the heart of their waiting God?

Idle are speculations before this proof of God's love for us. Do we ever stop to really think how endless is this lovemaking of God to the soul of man, his bride? In life, and after it, until he and she are forever united, the ingenuity of his love pursues her, offering ever-new tokens, new proofs of his infinite and divine love for her. No. Don't let us call them "poor souls." Let us call them holy souls, waiting souls, souls burning with love of God and begging us to hasten their reunion with him whom they have seen once already. The seeing and the delay of being one with him must indeed be purgatory.

Yet, why go to purgatory? One can bypass it. There is a choice and each one of us is given the joyous privilege to make it. Stainless must be our wedding garment when we come before the gaze of the Bridegroom. We can keep it white and pure from baptism to death, for his grace is always there to help us. But we are weak, weighed down with the flesh, the world, and the devil. We fall and stain our baptismal robes. But oh—the goodness of God! They can be washed clean, and for this he offers us the confessional, where, in utter abandonment of love, he washes them with his own Precious Blood. All that remains to us then, is to make up here and now, in this world, on this earth, the penance given to us by him through his priest.

It is so simple. Consider a mother and child. The mother goes shopping and cautions the child not to touch her favorite vase. When she returns, the vase is lying on the floor, broken into a thousand pieces, and the child runs to her, all sorrow, all contrition. Loving mother that she is, she understands and forgives, kissing the tears away, the just anger she felt upon first sight now all gone in her mother's love and gladness at knowing her child understands what he did and is sorry. Peace and love are restored again between them.

But a wise mother will not stop at that, for she will realize that the character of the child is to be shaped now, in childhood, for life. Quietly and slowly, she will impart the price, the penance to be paid for disobedience. Each week the child will give up part of his allowance, until the vase is paid for. Thus, the child, while basking in the light of his mother's love and forgiveness, will learn that for each disobedience or defalcation, there is a restitution.

You and I know, incidentally, that the mother will make all allowances on the price of the vase. Mothers are like that. And so is God, even to those in the land of twilight, in purgatory. Even there, he offers them the chance to have their sins atoned for completely by others—you and me—through the alms of our prayers and through the wealth of Masses said for them.

Consider November, then, the month of the dead, the month of prayers, as a family month. For isn't the whole Church—the Church living on earth, the Church suffering in purgatory and the Church triumphant in heaven—one big family? And should not the little family of Christ—husband, wife, and children—make November their special prayer month? For most of those who inhabit purgatory belong to some family on earth. The few who don't have family here receive the alms of prayers of their spiritual relatives—all Catholics.

The month of November should be a meditation month for husband and wife, for it is an object lesson of their whole vocation. They became man and wife to eschew purgatory, to bypass it altogether, to fly straight and true into the heart of Christ, our Tremendous Lover and to teach their children to bypass it and fly straight to him too. Little human family, little church of Christ, you have been called so to live that you enter the gates of heaven without stopping anywhere on the road to it! For yours is a vocation to love, and *love alone* is a nonstop express train to heaven.

You who are families, the schools of love, of saints-in-the-making, begin to make November your almsgiving month, your month of the great *caritas* (love) of God that bridges heaven and earth, purgatory and paradise. Make it a month of family prayers for all holy souls, those belonging to you and all of the others too. Then the holy souls will help you, in turn, to bypass purgatory altogether!

More of Catherine's Talks on Feastdays have been included in the following two publications by Madonna House:

Donkey Bells: Advent and Christmas, with Catherine Doherty. Gives customs and feast day information, stories and meditations for the season. A treasure for the family.

Season of Mercy: Lent and Easter, with Catherine Doherty. Gives Catherine's meditations from Ash Wednesday through Easter and up to Pentecost. Also a short section on Easter customs and traditions.

Resources

Church Teachings

The Catholic Church has addressed the needs and role of families in a wealth of wise teachings regarding marriage and family. Some of the major writings from recent years are listed below.

The Catechism of the Catholic Church. This excellent reference book is well-indexed, with concise, understandable information on all aspects of the Catholic faith, including marriage, family, and childrearing. Approved by Pope John Paul II, it is the first "universal" catechism in 400 years.

"The Role of the Christian Family in the Modern World" (*Familiaris Consortio*), Apostolic Exhortation of Pope John Paul II, 1981.

"Letter to Families," 1994; **"Letter to Women,"** 1995; and **"Letter to Children,"** 1994, by Pope John Paul II.

"The Truth and Meaning of Human Sexuality: Guidelines for Education within the Family," by the Pontifical Council for the Family, 1996.

"Pornography and Violence in the Communications Media," 1989; and **"Pastoral Instruction on the Means of Social Communication,"** 1971, by the Pontifical Council for Social Communications.

"Lay Members of Christ's Faithful People" (*Christifideles Laici*), Post-Synodal Apostolic Exhortation of Pope John Paul II, 1988.

"On the Dignity and Vocation of Woman" (*Mulieris Dignitatem*), Apostolic Letter by Pope John Paul II, 1988.

"Of Human Life" (*Humanae Vitae*), encyclical by Pope Paul VI, 1968.

Note: All the above Church documents are available from Pauline Books & Media.

141

Index

Other Writings by
Catherine de Hueck Doherty

Apostolic Farming
Dearly Beloved: 3 volumes
Dear Father
Dear Seminarian
Donkey Bells
Doubts, Loneliness, Rejection
Fragments of My Life
The Gospel of a Poor Woman
The Gospel without Compromise
Grace in Every Season
Journey Inward
Lubov
Molchanie
My Heart and I
My Russian Yesterdays
Not Without Parables
Our Lady's Unknown Mysteries
O Jesus
The People of the Towel and the Water
Poustinia
Re–entry into Faith
Season of Mercy
Sobornost
Soul of My Soul
Stations of the Cross
Strannik
Urodivoi
Welcome, Pilgrim

Available from:

Madonna House Publications
Combermere, Ontario, Canada
K0J 1L0
Web-site: http://www.mv.igs.net/~madonnah